HOW TO KEEP A COMPETITIVE EDGE IN THE TALENT GAME

This report is based on discussions within the CEPS Task Force on the Quantity and Quality of Human Capital in Higher Education: Comparing the EU, the US and China, chaired by Jan-Eric Sundgren, Senior Adviser to the CEO of Volvo and former President of Chalmers University of Technology in Gothenburg. The authors of this final report served as rapporteurs. Christal Morehouse is Senior Project Manager, Bertelsmann Stiftung. Matthias Busse is Researcher at CEPS.

The contents of the report reflect the general tone and direction of the discussions among the members of the Task Force (listed in the annex), but its recommendations do not necessarily represent a full common position agreed by all members. Nor do they necessarily represent the views of CEPS or the institutions to which the members belong.

The Centre for European Policy Studies (CEPS) is an independent policy research institute in Brussels. Its mission is to produce sound policy research leading to constructive solutions to the challenges facing Europe.

How to keep a competitive edge in the talent game

Lessons for the EU from China and the US

Christal Morehouse

and

Matthias Busse

Centre for European Policy Studies
Brussels

Rowman & Littlefield International
London • New York

Published by Rowman & Littlefield International, Ltd.
Unit A, Whitacre Mews, 26-34 Stannary Street, London SE11 4AB
www.rowmaninternational.com

Rowman & Littlefield International, Ltd. is an affiliate of Rowman & Littlefield
4501 Forbes Boulevard, Suite 200, Lanham, Maryland 20706, USA
With additional offices in Boulder, New York, Toronto (Canada), and Plymouth (UK)
www.rowman.com

Centre for European Policy Studies
Place du Congrès 1, B-1000 Brussels
Tel: (32.2) 229.39.11 Fax: (32.2) 219.41.51
E-mail: info@ceps.eu
Website: http://www.ceps.eu

British Library Cataloguing in Publication Data
A catalogue record for this book is available from the British Library

ISBN 978-1-78348-298-6

Library of Congress Cataloging-in-Publication Data Available

TABLE OF CONTENTS

LIST OF FIGURES AND TABLES

FOREWORD

The state of higher education provides a reflection of the state of a society and its economic prospects. A modern economy cannot remain competitive in a changing and interconnected world if it cannot count on a well-educated work force. The topic tackled by the CEPS Task Force on the Quantity and Quality of Human Capital in Higher Education is thus central for the future of the world's three largest economies – the EU, the US and China. This report makes a unique contribution by providing European policy-makers with a view of the global landscape in higher education and a mirror in which they can see their own failings and successes.

Most decisions on higher education are taken at the national, and sometimes even regional, level without taking this global environment into account. But this is short-sighted because European graduates will have to compete with their counterparts around the globe in the same way that European companies will have to compete in a global market for talent.

That the US is the undisputed leader in creating top-level universities is widely known. This report shows, however, that China is engaged in a rapid catching-up process, initially in terms of quantity, but there are first signs that its universities might soon become a serious competitor in terms of quality. This should not be surprising given the thousand-year-old tradition of learning in China. But it should be a wake-up call for Europe that the continent where universities first emerged (at least according to European historians) now risks being beaten not only by its own offspring on the other side of the Atlantic, but being relegated to third place.

Such an outcome can be avoided since European universities appear in substantial numbers in the medium-to-high categories. The challenge for Europe is not only to maintain the average level, but also to add elements of what this report calls 'premium class'.

The one 'dog that did not bark' in this story is India, which is home to an ever-growing young population with younger cohorts who will outstrip in pure numbers those of China by a large margin, given the much higher birth rates of India. Progress in education in India has been spotty, however, including in the area of higher education. This is surprising because of the widespread image of India as an exporter of IT services. But few Indian universities appear in the global rankings and it is symptomatic that India does not participate in global comparative studies like PISA (Programme for International Student Assessment), conducted by the Organisation for Economic Cooperation and Development (OECD). Two Indian states participated only once in PISA, but their pupils were ranked at the very bottom of the over 100 nations that participated. The Indian authorities then decided not to participate anymore in PISA, citing a 'cultural bias'. This is a pity and does not augur well for the economic future of the largest democracy on earth.

Daniel Gros
Director of CEPS

PREFACE

This report attempts to capture the ideas, debate and policy recommendations that emerged from the discussions within the CEPS Task Force on the Quantity and Quality of Human Capital in Higher Education: Comparing the EU, the US and China. The group met in full-day sessions on four occasions between April 2013 and June 2014.

The Task Force was conducted with the participation of the European Commission (DG Joint Research Centre, DG Research and Innovation, DG Education and Culture), the European Institute of Technology, the European Investment Bank, the European University Association, the European Round Table of Industrialists, the European Schoolnet, the Bertelsmann Foundation, the Confederation of Danish Industry, Hyundai, Mitsui, Siemens and Volvo. Invited speakers included specialists from the Centre for Higher Education, UCL Amsterdam, the European Parliament and DG Education and Culture. The full list of Task Force members and invited speakers can be found in the annex.

The Task Force's Report is based on original research and draws upon the existing literature and available data. It has benefited greatly from the expertise of the Task Force members, which was contributed during the meetings and related exchanges. We would also like to thank Felix Roth who, during his time as Research Fellow at CEPS, started the Task Force and provided valuable input. Finally we would like thank Jan-Eric Sundgren, Senior Adviser to the CEO at Volvo, for his skilful chairing of the Task Force meetings, ensuring that discussions remained focused and that its recommendations to policy-makers were well-grounded and feasible.

Christal Morehouse
and
Matthias Busse

EXECUTIVE SUMMARY

This Task Force Report compares tertiary education in the European Union, the United States and China. Identifying the respective advantages of the US and China over the EU reveals an urgent need for Europe to adapt to international competition in attracting and developing talent and making the most of the existing domestic talent pool. Failure to take such action jeopardises Europe's prospects for economic growth and prosperity in future. Investment in education, excellent performance in international rankings and keeping pace with technological change are essential if the EU wishes to maintain its economic and political status in a rapidly changing globalised world. In many respects, the EU has the proper tools to become more attractive to foreign talent, but it needs to apply them in a purposeful.

The aim of this analysis is to determine how the EU as a region compares with respect to the US and China, how to improve higher education in the EU and how to secure its stock of human capital. By 2020, the global map of higher education will be completely redrawn. By 2030, China will emerge as the world's largest source of brainpower. In 2000, the US and China were global equals, each home to 17% of 25- to 34-year-olds with a tertiary degree, i.e. university-level, in OECD and G20 countries. This cohort was chosen since tertiary education is usually completed before the age of 26, and thus this age group catches the youngest cohort entering the tertiary-educated workforce. In 2010, China emerged as the single leader of this cohort and is expected to become home to 29% of the world's tertiary-degree holders by 2020, will dominate the 'brain game' *quantitatively*.

Looking at the *quality* of education, the 'brain race' is harder to gauge. The 'brain race' is fuelled by universities but the public and private sectors must also foster the development of skills. Global talent mobility is part of the international skill balance, as is the employability of graduates. It is still unclear which nations will emerge as global leaders in the coming decades. The world is changing rapidly, and the absence of progress is the equivalent of decline. In the 'brain race', countries will have to run to stand still, and they will have to progress very quickly if they want to emerge as global talent leaders.

There are a number of game-changing factors affecting higher education and this report investigates the most salient among them. These include how digital technology is integrated into education, how education relates to employment and how tertiary institutions are governed.

Viewed intra-regionally, Europe is making progress in developing its talent pipeline. Yet if we take a step back and set the EU in the context of how the US and China are faring – and are likely to fare in the future – there are lessons to be learned. The EU must remain competitive in the emerging knowledge-based global economy by strategically growing its talent pipeline. With this aim in mind, the EU and its member states should:

- conduct research into the state of human capital,
- create incentives to counteract a depletion of skills and to develop talent,
- make investments that increase the positive impact of competence on economies and societies, and
- increase the relevance of tertiary education for the labour market and life chances.

Such actions could be thought of as contributing to 'virtuous circles' of talent and innovation to sustain prosperity and growth and to secure the long-term well-being and quality of life in Europe.

1. INTRODUCTION

This book examines education at the university (or tertiary) level in the European Union, the United States and China. The aim of this analysis is to determine how well the EU as a region performs with respect to the US and China and how to improve higher education in the EU – and with it the EU's stock of human capital.

The skills, abilities and innovative capacity of European citizens are vital to competitiveness of European economies. Data from the Organisation for Economic Cooperation and Development (OECD) have repeatedly shown a positive correlation between high levels of tertiary education and employment, earnings, innovation and economic prosperity. We no longer live in an industrial age in which amassing financial capital alone is enough to attract the manpower and – most importantly – the brainpower that economies need to create jobs and growth. Some have suggested that our current period could best be dubbed the 'talent era', in which the balance of economic strength might be tipped in favour of those countries that are strong innovators. And for innovation, one needs a healthy stock of human capital.

The so-called 'brain race' is fuelled by universities; the public and private sectors must also foster the development of skills. Global talent mobility is part of the international talent balance, as is the employability of graduates. It is still unclear which nations will emerge as the global leaders in the coming decades. The world is changing rapidly, and a lack of progress can spell decline. In the 'brain race', countries will have to run to stand still and they will have to progress very quickly if they want to emerge as global talent leaders.

The EU has recognised the role of tertiary education as a benchmark for overall prosperity and long-term economic growth in Europe. The

Europe 2020 Strategy (European Commission, 2010a),[1] set the goal of increasing the tertiary graduation rate among 30- to 34-year-olds to 40%. The EU has also established scoreboards (such as the EU Innovation Scoreboard and the EU Higher Education Mobility Scoreboard) in a number of areas. These scoreboards include information on how Europe's most precious resource – human capital – is changing. Viewed intra-regionally, Europe is making progress in developing its talent pipeline. But if we take a step back and set the EU in the context of how the US and China are doing – and are likely to do in the future – several lessons can be drawn. The EU must remain competitive in the emerging knowledge-based global economy by strategically growing its talent pipeline. With this aim in mind, the EU and its member states should:

- conduct in-depth research into the state of human capital in the region,
- create incentives to counteract a depletion of skills and to develop talent,
- make investments that increase the positive impact of competence on economies and societies, and
- increase the relevance of tertiary education for the labour market and life chances.

Such elements could be thought of as contributing to 'virtuous circles' of talent and innovation to sustain prosperity and growth.

The remainder of this report is organised around four chapters. Chapter 2 offers a comparative analysis of the performance of the EU, the US and China in higher education and assesses the quality and quantity of education delivered by their respective institutions. Indicators, such as the number of tertiary degree holders and the reputation of universities, are examined in a comparative manner. This chapter considers past

---

[1] Adopted in 2010, Europe 2020 was the EU's growth strategy for becoming a "smart, sustainable and inclusive economy" over the next decade, in the hope that these three mutually reinforcing priorities would help the EU and the member states achieve high levels of employment, productivity and social cohesion.

performance and also uses data on upper-secondary education (e.g. performance of future tertiary classes) to project, how one might expect higher education to 'perform' in the coming years.

Chapter 3, entitled "Private and public funding of higher education in the EU, the US and China", investigates investment in education in the EU, the US and in China. It not only examines the aggregate funding for institutions of higher learning, but it also breaks down the composition (private and public) of this funding. Like chapter 2, this chapter explores past trends and consider how changes in funding could affect higher education in the coming years.

Chapter 4, entitled "Game-changing factors in innovating higher education", explores the impact of technology, the employability of skills, as well as university governance on tertiary education.

Each chapter of this report distils policy recommendations from the analysis. The concluding chapter 5 draws together the chapter recommendations and places them in a broader policy context. Four sets of recommendations are addressed to EU policy-makers with the aim of improving higher education in the EU and the EU's stock of human capital to ensure its continued competitiveness in the global economy.

2. COMPARATIVE PERFORMANCE OF THE EU, THE US AND CHINA IN HIGHER EDUCATION

In an ever-smaller world, how countries perform in relation to one another is an important indicator of their future prospects for economic and social development. This chapter compares tertiary education outcomes in the European Union, the United States and China by closely examining the quantity and quality of higher education. Because upper secondary schools 'feed' into the university system, the quality of their performance is also taken into account. Analysing pre-secondary education performance and its impact on human capital would go beyond the scope of this report. It is nevertheless acknowledged that investment in education at an early age yields a high return to the quality of human capital (Carneiro & Heckman, 2003).

Concerning the quantity of education, China is making rapid progress towards becoming a hub for highly educated persons. According to the OECD (2012a), "if current trends continue, China and India will account for 40 percent of all young people with a tertiary education in G20 and OECD countries by the year 2020, while the United States and European Union countries will account for just over a quarter". Even though a lower percentage of China's population will graduate from higher education than that of the US and the EU, the sheer scale of China's population will allow it to dominate the brain pool. China has been investing heavily in its educational systems, and OECD projections for 2020 show that the country could achieve a tertiary graduation rate of 27%, which is below the EU average but higher than the current Italian rate.

The US is far from the global leader in tertiary graduation rates, ranking 12th in the world. Korea ranks first with a tertiary attainment rate among 25- to 34-year-olds of 64% (OECD, 2012a). In 2013, most EU countries had achieved a graduation rate of 37% of 25- to 34-year-olds (Eurostat, 2014a), which falls just under the US rate (43% in 2011) (OECD, 2012a). EU countries that have not yet achieved such a high graduation rate either possess a very efficient system of vocational training, such as Germany and Austria, or are making reasonable progress towards achieving the target. Italy for example, has rapidly increased its national graduation rate in the last three decades.

Concerning the quality of education, there is no international standard for comparing the quality of university student performance. The OECD has been developing a project on the Assessment of Higher Education Learning Outcomes (AHELO), which aims to assess what tertiary-educated graduates in 17 countries and regions know. The AHELO test was designed to evaluate general skills (such as critical thinking, analytical reasoning, problem-solving and written communication), economics and engineering. It is intended to be administered shortly before graduation from undergraduate studies (Tremblay et al., 2012). The project has struggled with the design of its assessment tool and has worked through several consultations with stakeholders to come up with a feasible design.

The performance of upper-secondary students on the well-known PISA test,[2] in combination with university reputation (rankings), help define the contours of the quality of tertiary education in international comparisons. Generally EU students outperform their US counterparts in the PISA study. And although the quality of education is thought to vary greatly across China, Shanghai and Hong Kong were the global

---

[2] The Programme for International Student Assessment (PISA) is a worldwide test administered by the OECD (Organisation for Economic Cooperation and Development) of the scholastic performance of 15-year-old students in mathematics, science and reading. It was first performed in 2000 and is repeated every three years in both member and non-member countries, with the aim of improving educational policies and outcomes.

benchmarks in the most recent (2012) PISA ranking. Regarding the reputation of universities world-wide,[3] US universities dominate the top global rankings. In the EU, the United Kingdom stands out as a strong global competitor in the tertiary education sector. Continental Europe, however, lags behind the US and is losing ground to Chinese universities. Germany's top-performing university (Ludwig-Maximilians-Universität München) came in, at 55th place, behind China's top performers – University of Hong Kong (43rd place), Peking University (45th place) and Tsinghua University (50th place). France's top performer (École Normale Supérieure) was ranked 65th and Spain's best university (Pompeu Fabra University - Barcelona), at 164th place, came in behind no fewer than five Chinese universities (University of Hong Kong, Peking University, Tsinghua University, Hong Kong University of Science and Technology and Chinese University of Hong Kong). Evidence suggests that China will soon be able to increase its presence in university rankings and – in addition to its domestic talent, its growing economy and the reputation of its universities – attract talent from abroad.

This chapter is based on the following data sets:

- Share in global stock of 25- to 34 year-olds with a tertiary degree in 2000, 2010 and projected for 2020;
- First[4] university degrees in science and engineering by region, 2010;
- Total numbers of first university degrees in engineering, 2000-10;
- Various global university-wide rankings, 2013 and 2014; and
- PISA results, 2012.

---

[3] Based on the Times Higher Education World University Rankings 2013-2014.
[4] Second degrees are not included in these statistics.

2.1 The quantity of education at the tertiary and upper-secondary level

2.1.1 The quantity of tertiary graduates across OECD and G20 countries

The correlation between high levels of education and innovation, economic growth and long-term prosperity is strong. Therefore, the EU must develop a talent strategy in which tertiary education serves as the cornerstone. It has already taken steps to do so. For example, the European Commission's 'Europe 2020' strategy has set a target of 40% for the tertiary graduation rate for 30-34 year olds by the end of this decade. A number of EU member states had already met, or surpassed this benchmark in 2012: Belgium, Cyprus, Denmark, Finland, France, Ireland, Lithuania, Luxembourg, the Netherlands, Spain, Sweden and the UK. Taken on its own, this appears to be good news, but if we compare the development and projected output of Europe's strongest producers of tertiary graduates – France, Germany, the UK and Spain – with the US and China, a different picture emerges.

By 2020, the global map of higher education will be completely redrawn. The number of people with a tertiary-level education in OECD and G20 countries is expected to have grown from 91 million 25- to 34-year-olds in 2000 to 204 million (OECD, 2012a). Within 20 years, China will emerge as the world's largest source of brainpower. This shift is unprecedented in human history, especially when one considers that in 2000, the United States and China were producing the same share of global graduates, 17% each (OECD, 2012a). In 2010 China emerged as the single leader of this cohort. China is expected to become home to 29% of the world's tertiary-degree holders in 2020 and will dominate the 'brain game' quantitatively. In 2020, China will have more than double the share of 25- to 34-year-old tertiary degree holders in OECD and G20 countries, as compared to its closest competitor India (12%). The United States is expected to have the third-largest percentage at 11%.

Both the US and China are pursuing benchmarks to expand their talent pools. Obviously the individual performance of these two countries cannot be measured by their share in the global talent pool, but rather by the size relative to their population. Nevertheless, the changes in the global stocks are crucial in determining where future skilled labour supply will reside. Indeed, China's progress in increasing the share of its population with a tertiary degree is impressive.

According to the OECD (2012a), it "has quintupled its number of tertiary graduates and doubled its number of tertiary institutions in the last 10 years". China has a National Plan for Medium- and Long-term Education Reform and Development. It aims to increase the number of its citizens with higher education from 98.3 million in 2009 to 195 million in 2020 (OECD, 2012a). The country's leadership would like to shift the economy from a labour-intensive one to a knowledge-based economy. Beyond developing talent domestically, China plans increasingly to recruit talent from abroad, using its universities to attract students. In 2009, the US government aimed to help the country become the nation "with the highest proportion of 25- to 34-year-old university graduates by 2020" (OECD, 2012a). To meet this goal, it would need to have 60% of that age cohort graduate by the end of this decade. As countries of very different size compete in the global brain game, smaller countries may face new challenges regarding the advantages and risks of workforce concentration vs. diversification.

Figure 1. Share in global stock* of 25- to 34 year-olds with a tertiary degree, 2000, 2010 and projected for 2020

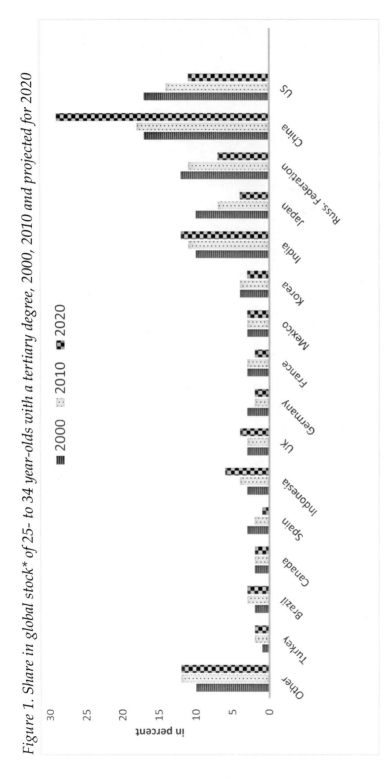

* Global is here represented by OECD and other G20 countries, due to lack of data on other countries.

Notes: Projections presented in this chart do not take into account policy measures being pursued in some countries to increase higher education attainment.

Sources: Authors' configuration based on data from the OECD Database, UNESCO and national statistics websites for Argentina, China, India, Indonesia, Saudi Arabia and South Africa.

Within the EU, the UK is forecast to be best positioned to compete for international students in the future. The country is expected to increase slightly its share of global tertiary graduates in 2020, which is contrary to the trend in other EU countries. Models for predicting international student mobility use indicators such as: income per capita, demographic change, domestic and international higher education participation rates, as well as the perceived quality of education and employment prospects for the degree acquired (Böhm et al., 2004). Language is also thought to be an important factor for international students when they choose an international destination. International students often prefer courses taught in English.

Recommendation

Measuring the quantity of education in global comparison

The EU's tertiary education benchmark, embedded in the Europe 2020 strategy, aims to increase the EU's tertiary graduation rate among 30- to 34-year-olds to 40%. This benchmark should be reported on in *global comparison*, and the progress of EU member states should be discussed regularly by the responsible ministers from EU member states in a global – not just an intra-EU – context. This might be done with reference to non-EU countries that are expected to have the world's highest numbers of graduates, such as China, or those such as Korea that have a large percentage of their population graduating from universities.

2.1.2 The quantity of scarce talent: Graduates of science and engineering

One area of education is expected to affect the global 'brain balance' and national labour markets disproportionately, and with it, a country's ability to innovate. This area is STEM: Science, Technology, Engineering and Mathematics. STEM skills are some of the most difficult and time-consuming to acquire. They tend to attract smaller numbers than are needed to satisfy labour demand in many countries. Furthermore, the science and technology occupations comprise an increasing share of total employment across OECD and G20 countries. And this shift in skills demand is expected to continue as emerging economies become knowledge-based.

The *Science and Engineering Indicators 2012* report estimates that 5.5 million first university degrees in science and engineering were earned around the globe in 2010. The distribution of these degrees among regions was uneven: "almost a quarter of those degrees were conferred in China (24 percent), 17 percent in the EU and 10 percent in the United States" (National Science Board, 2014). The rate of increase in these types of degrees in the past decade has been strong in both the EU and the US, but only if one compares these regions to the world without China. For example, Germany doubled the number of science and engineering graduates between 2000 and 2010, from 67,000 to 139,000. The US increased its first degree science and engineering holder cohort from: 399,000 to 525,000. In the same period China more than trebled its stock of such first degree holders, from 359,000 to 1,300,000 degrees (National Science Board, 2014). The rapid skill-pool upgrade in science and engineering is historically unprecedented. This strong skill growth has to do with the share of students that opt for such studies: "whereas 5 percent of all bachelor's degrees awarded in the United States were in engineering, 31 percent of such degrees in China were in this field" (National Science Board, 2014). China is likely to maintain its newly established position as the world's leading source of new science and engineering graduates.

Figure 2. First university degrees in science and engineering by region, 2010 (thousands)

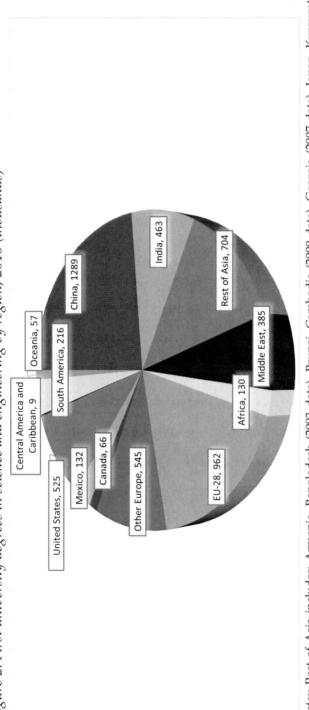

Notes: Rest of Asia includes: Armenia, Bangladesh (2003 data), Brunei, Cambodia (2009 data), Georgia (2007 data), Japan, Kyrgyzstan, Malaysia (2009 data), Mongolia, Singapore, South Korea and Taiwan; Africa includes: Algeria (data 2007), Burundi (2004 data), Cameroon (2008 data), Eritrea, Ethiopia, Ghana (2009 data), Kenya (2001 data), Lesotho (2003 data), Madagascar, Morocco, Mozambique (2011 data), Namibia (2008 data), Swaziland (2006 data) and Uganda (2004 data); EU-28: France (2009 data), Luxemburg (2008 data) and no data for Malta; Central America and the Caribbean includes: El Salvador, Guatemala (2007 data), Honduras (2003 data) and Panama; South America includes: Argentina (2009 data), Bolivia (2000 data), Brazil, Chile, Colombia, Guyana, Uruguay, Venezuela (2004 data); and data for India are 2003.

Source: Authors' configuration based on data from National Science Board (2014).

Figure 3. Total numbers of first university degrees in science and engineering, 2000-10

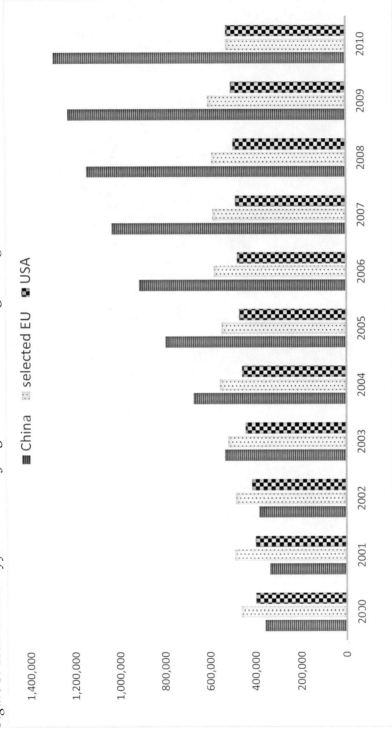

Notes: EU data from countries producing the largest cohorts: Germany, France, Italy, Spain, Poland and the UK. No data are available for France for 2010.

Source: Authors' configuration based on data from National Science Board (2014).

The targeted up-skilling of a population in the areas of science and engineering is not a goal in itself. This makes sense because current economic trends surrounding job creation, destruction and innovation show that graduate absorption rates in this area are high and that demand for such skills is growing. For example, shortage occupation lists in the EU such as in the UK, Germany and Austria, which allow for the immigration of workers with scarce skills in selected professions, are all dominated at the high-skill end by STEM-based occupations. [5] And according to the OECD, in most member countries, science and technology professionals "represented more than a quarter of total employment in 2010. The share was over 40 percent in Luxembourg, Sweden, Denmark and Switzerland" (OECD, 2011b). Additionally, there has been an impressive rate of increase in employment in science and technology: "between 1998 and 2008, employment in HRST [human resources in science and technology] occupations increased at a faster rate than total employment in all OECD and G20 countries with available data" (OECD, 2012a).

The private sector in EU member states has made significant contributions to improving the skill base there, including in STEM. For example, the University Business Cooperation has been developed in a joint effort between the private sector and the European Commission to achieve this aim and to examine the relationship between skills and employment. As part of the Cooperation, the University Business Forum meets regularly. It is: "an annual forum that brings together higher education institutions, companies, business associations, intermediaries and public authorities, providing them with a common space at a European level for dialogue, networking and the exchange of good practice" (European Commission, 2014d).

---

[5] For further information, see UK Department of Visas and Immigration (2014), Bundesministerium für Wirtschaft und Energie et al. (2014) and Bundesministerium für Arbeit, Soziales, Konsumentenschutz (2014).

Recommendation

Prevent STEM-skill depletion.

The EU, EU member states and the private sector have increased their efforts to encourage the development of STEM skills, especially by fostering intra-EU projects. These initiatives should be expanded through exchanges beyond Europe. Countries such as China, India and the US, with large STEM programmes and skill cohorts, should be considered as partners with which to work with more strategically. Private-sector involvement in fostering STEM the acquisition of skills has two important components: ensuring that the skills acquired match current labour-market standards and motivating students to learn skills that lead to promising employment opportunities by introducing them into workplaces during their studies.

2.2 The quality of education at the tertiary and upper-secondary level

There is no international standard for comparing the quality of university-student performance, although the OECD has been working on such an assessment tool in their AHELO programme. But the OECD has faced considerable challenges in developing this tool. A persistent problem that the OECD has tried to remedy in feasibility studies is how to best assess knowledge and skills in a standardised test, when regional learning and testing cultures differ to a great extent. The OECD has yet to find a satisfactory solution to this problem. In the absence of internationally comparative assessments of tertiary learning, university rankings and the performance of upper secondary students on the PISA test provide some internationally comparative data on the quality of tertiary education and on the pipeline of talent that is 'feeding' into the higher education system.

2.2.1 Global university-wide rankings

This section looks at four[6] global university-wide rankings: the Times Higher Education ranking (Times Higher Education, 2014a), the Academic Ranking of World Universities, referred to as the Shanghai Ranking (Center for World-Class Universities of Shanghai Jiao Tong University, 2014a), the Quacquarelli Symonds World University Rankings, referred to as the QS Ranking, (Quacquarelli Symonds, 2014a) and the Webometrics Ranking (Consejo Superior de Investigaciones Científicas 2014). It examines what these rankings tell us about the reputations of EU, the US and Chinese institutions of higher education. It also looks at the methodology employed in producing these rankings.

Rankings are highly influential because they can define a university's reputation. They often act as a proxy for university performance in public debate, because of a lack of better internationally comparative data on university performance. They come in several forms, such as university-wide rankings, or faculty rankings. Europe is home to over 3,000 institutions of higher education; globally, there are around 22,000 (Consejo Superior de Investigaciones Científicas, 2014). China's higher education sector has been growing and consists of around 2,500 institutions (Ministry of Education of the People's Republic of China, 2013).

With such a large number of tertiary institutions worldwide, it is hard to find the vocabulary to accurately describe performance-tier-groups in higher education. For example, one could argue that the top 500 institutions worldwide are all top-tier because they are ranked well within the top 3% of all universities internationally. Or one could posit that only the top 10 or 20 institutions should be considered top-tier, because only a very short list of institutions attain the critical mass of

---

[6] There are other international university rankings that this paper does not consider. The purpose of this paper is to analyse the general trends in universities' reputations that are reflected through a selection of several prominent global ranking systems.

prestige required to motivate students, businesses and policy-makers alike to 'buy into' them.

In the context of this paper, the following vocabulary will provide a framework for roughly tier-grouping tertiary institutions:

- *Premium class*: Institutions that score in the top 20. These are universities that are household names and able to skim off the world's brightest students. These institutions are so reputable that stakeholders from the private and public sector compete to buy into them.
- *Very good*: Universities that finish within the top 21 to 100. These are higher learning providers that are able to positively brand their university with reference to global rankings.
- *Good*: Universities that place within the top 101 to 500 institutions worldwide. These universities can use their reputations as an asset (when competing for students and funding) and have raised their international profiles through the rankings.
- *The rest*: These are institutions that place outside the top 500. Thus their reputation is arguably not meaningfully impacted by the rankings, as they are not mentioned in many of them, or one has to scroll through a multitude of institutions to find them.

University rankings are, at best, a weak proxy for gauging the quality of tertiary education. A lot of literature has been devoted to the shortcomings of various university rankings. For the purposes of this section, only three issues will be touched upon as indicative of the challenges facing global university-wide ranking systems. First, tertiary institutions are diverse and in many cases one can't compare them in a meaningful way. For example, one can't adequately evaluate a music conservatory and an engineering school using one set of criteria. Second, organisations that rank universities don't have the resources to collect and evaluate a large set of comparative criteria in depth; consequently breadth and depth tend to be traded offs. And third, some countries have tertiary educational institutions that offer university-level learning environments, but are excluded from the rankings because of their country-specific (internationally non-standard) institutional set-ups, resulting in an under-representation of the national tertiary sector. The International Ranking Expert Group (IREG), set up by the UNESCO European Centre for Higher Education and the Institute for Higher Education Policy, has been working for a decade to improve the quality of higher education league tables and rankings (International Ranking Expert Group, 2006).

Each of the four university ranking systems examined in this section has its own set of indicators (indeed each ranking may have several sets of indicators for the various typologies of rankings it conducts). The Times Higher Education ranking uses 13 indicators and clusters these into the following five weighted areas of performance: teaching (30%), research (30%), citations (30%), industry income (2.5%) and international outlook (7.5%) (Times Higher Education, 2014b). The Shanghai Ranking applies six indicators grouped into the following four weighted categories: quality of education (10%), quality of faculty (40%), research output (40%) and per capita performance (10%) (Center for World-Class Universities of Shanghai Jiao Tong University, 2014b). The QS World University Rankings (which used to be conducted together with the Times Higher Education ranking, but have been independent since 2010) uses the following indicators: academic reputation (40%), employer reputation (10%), faculty-student ratio (20%), citations per faculty (20%), portion of international students (5%) and portion of international faculty (5%) (Quacquarelli Symonds, 2014b). The Webometrics Ranking assumes that a university's web presence mirrors its performance. It uses a university website's visibility (50%) and website activity (50%) as the basis for its ranking.

However, the data sets that feed into the indicators of various university-wide ranking systems do not always coincide with a prospective student's conception of what constitutes an accurate depiction of an institution's educational performance. The student is obliged to search in the methodology to understand what proxy has been chosen. For example, the quality of education criterion is measured by alumni achievement in the Shanghai ranking: "The total number of the alumni of an institution winning Nobel Prizes and Fields Medals" (Center for World-Class Universities of Shanghai Jiao Tong University, 2014b). The quality of teaching in the Times Higher Education ranking is measured by the student-teacher ratio and awarded degrees (among other things).

Despite diverse methodologies, the global narrative reflected in all four university rankings is clear: the US is the unrivalled global leader regarding the reputation of its tertiary 'premium-class' institutions. In the EU, the United Kingdom stands out as an international contender in this segment. In the top 100 universities (the 'premium' and 'very good' institutions taken together), the EU rivals the US, but comes in second in the majority of the rankings examined in this section. A small number of Chinese 'flagship' universities compete among the top 100 tertiary institutions in some of the selected rankings. Within the top 500 universities, the EU becomes the global leader across the four rankings. This region takes the lead, beginning with the top 100 to 300 range, depending on the ranking. Chinese universities are underrepresented in the four global rankings (with respect to the number of universities in the country) in all performance-tiers. Yet in some of the rankings, a few top-performing Chinese universities are climbing the tables and coming ahead of a number of the EU member states' best universities.

In the Times Higher Education ranking, Germany's top-performing university came in behind China at number 55, France's top performer was ranked 65 and Spain's best university (ranked 164) came in after no fewer than five Chinese universities. Europe is a global leader in the top 300 to 500. The results of this ranking suggest that China's universities have not gained broad recognition internationally, with some notable exceptions. Chinese universities seem to be gaining ground, with two universities in the top 50 and ten in the top 500, according to the Times Higher Education ranking (Times Higher Education, 2014a).

Figure 4. The Times Higher Education ranking, 2013-14

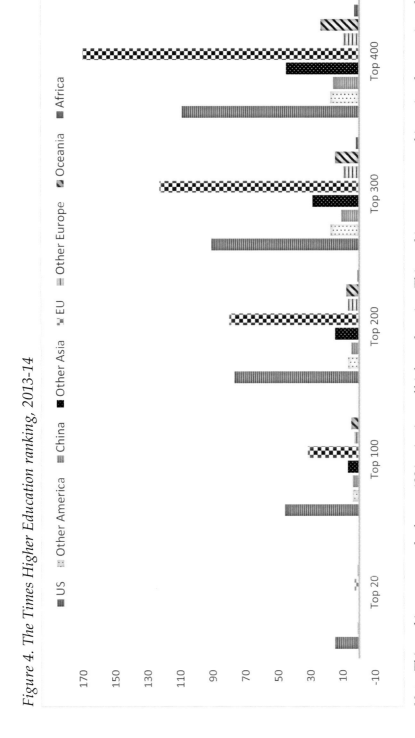

Notes: This ranking covers only the top 400 institutions of higher education. This ranking uses geographic regional categories, placing for example Turkey and Israel in 'Asia'. Its regional breakdown does not include the Middle East.

Source: Authors' configuration based on data from Times Higher Education (2014a).

If this trend continues, one might expect China to enter the 'premium' education sector and increase its presence among the 'very good' universities, thanks both to domestic talent and its ability to attract talent from abroad.

In the Shanghai ranking (shown in Figure 5), US universities also clearly dominate the 'premium class'. All 17 are from the US. Of the three European universities in the top 20, two are UK universities and one is Swiss. European universities place second to the US in the top-100 range and take the lead in the top-300 to -500 range. The Shanghai Ranking demonstrates that some EU member states do not have any universities ranked in the top-100 institutions: Italy, Austria, Spain, Ireland, the Czech Republic, Portugal, Greece, Poland, Hungary and Slovenia (Center for World-Class Universities of Shanghai Jiao Tong University, 2014a). China's universities have trouble competing among the 'premium class' and the 'very good' institutions in this ranking, with no universities ranked in the top 100. In the top 200, 300, 400 and 500, it had: 7, 13, 26 and 42 universities included, respectively (Center for World-Class Universities of Shanghai Jiao Tong University, 2014a).

The QS ranking (see Figure 6) shows a different distribution of universities, but the trend remains similar, with the US dominating the 'premium' higher education segment. In this ranking EU universities take the lead earlier to become the global leader among the top-100 universities, holding this position in the top-200, 300, 400 and 500 range.

The Webometrics ranking (see Figure 7), conducted by Spain's largest public research group – the Consejo Superior de Investigaciones Científicas (CSIC) – is a broad but shallow ranking of over 21,000 institutions worldwide based on their web presence and web activity. It too reflects similar trends among higher education institutions.

Of the top-20 ranked universities, only two are non-US institutions and again these are UK universities. The EU and the US clearly lead the rankings in the top 200, with the US ahead. The EU begins to dominate the rankings in the 300 to 500 top universities range.

Figure 5. The academic ranking of world universities (Shanghai ranking) by region, 2013

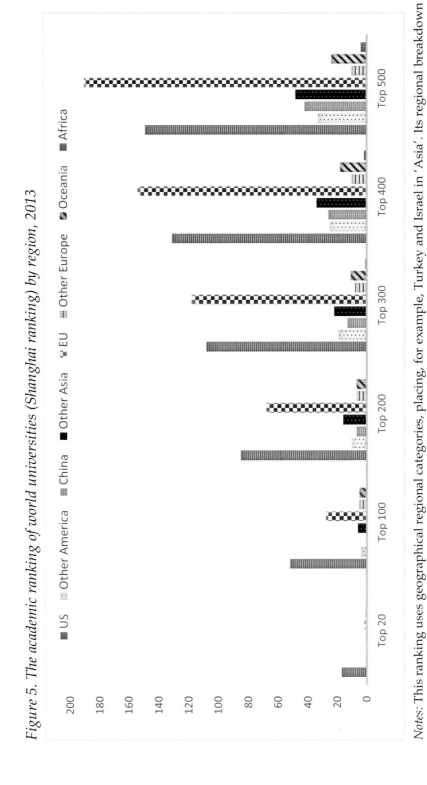

Notes: This ranking uses geographical regional categories, placing, for example, Turkey and Israel in 'Asia'. Its regional breakdown does not include the Middle East.

Source: Authors' configuration based on data from Center for World-Class Universities of Shanghai Jiao Tong University (2014a).

Figure 6. The QS world university rankings, 2013

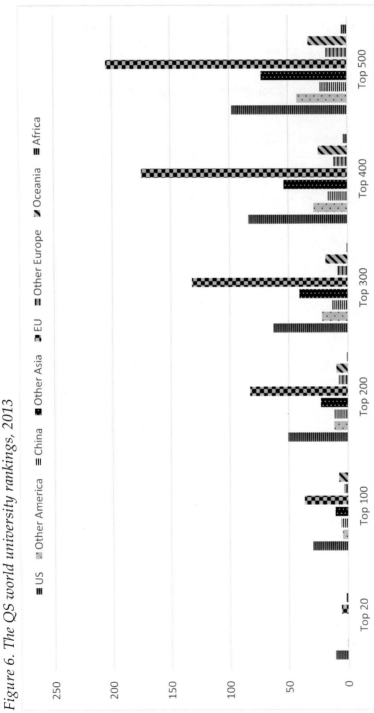

Notes: This ranking uses geographic regional categories, placing, for example, Turkey and Israel in 'Asia'. Its regional breakdown does not include the Middle East.

Source: Authors' configuration based on data from Quacquarelli Symonds (2014a).

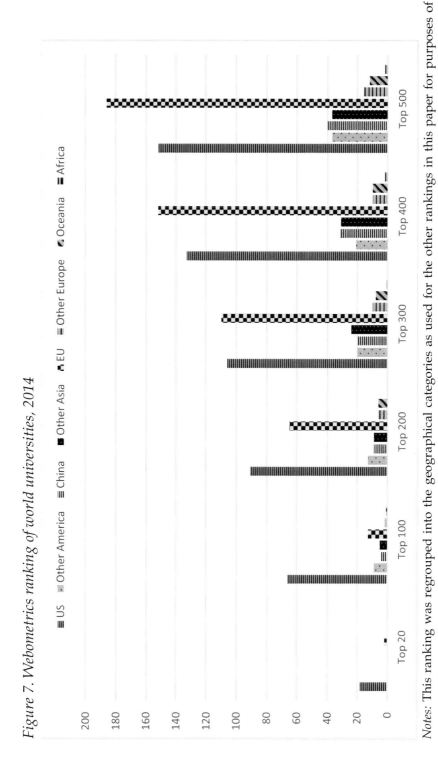

Figure 7. Webometrics ranking of world universities, 2014

Notes: This ranking was regrouped into the geographical categories as used for the other rankings in this paper for purposes of comparability.

Source: Authors' configuration based on data from Consejo Superior de Investigaciones Científicas (2014).

With the caveat that all existing university-wide rankings are a weak proxy for measuring university performance, they indicate that the EU is a 'very good' to 'good' performer on the global higher education stage. Yet what the EU seems to lack are sufficient flagship universities that rank in the 'premium class'. And among the 'very good' performers, some EU member states are completely missing from the charts.

What this analysis suggests is that there is room for improvement in facilitating student-university matching through comparative data and institutional transparency. One new ranking has emerged that aims to improve the quality of university evaluations and to make them more relevant for students as well as for other stakeholders. This is the U-Multirank initiative, which was launched in May 2014. It currently covers over 850 tertiary institutions around the world.

The U-Multirank website allows for a comparison of universities as a whole, as well as in four subject areas: physics, electrical engineering, mechanical engineering and business. In the future, it plans to expand the number of subject areas that one can compare. In 2015, the U-Multirank will be available also for psychology, computer science and medicine. The number of actively participating institutions covered is targeted to increase to 1,000 by 2017. The tool evaluates 30 indicators. They are clustered into the groups: teaching and learning, research, knowledge transfer, international orientation, regional engagement and 'general'.

Recommendation

Improve transparency in university performance.

The European Commission has provided seed funding for the multi-dimensional university assessment tool U-Multirank. This assessment tool has overcome some of the shortfalls of some university rankings. The Commission should work strongly with the private sector and foundations to ensure the longstanding operation of U-Multirank.

2.2.2 *PISA and the quality of upper-secondary education*

The most recent PISA results have challenged the conventional wisdom on which parts of the world incubate the smartest cohorts. But putting aside for a moment the differences in educational philosophies, it is clear which countries and regions are producing the best testable knowledge and skills around the globe. And in sharp contrast to what university rankings tell us about where the brainpower may be concentrated, PISA places the US below the OECD average, between Italy and Latvia. Only a few of China's leading regions were tested and these are among the PISA contenders that set the global benchmark regarding upper-secondary education.

Shanghai was indeed the best performer in 2012. Hong Kong came in third. EU member states showed large variations in performance. While students in Finland and Estonia proved competitive with the world's best performers, Romanian and Bulgarian students were among the poorest performers. If PISA is an indicator of future brainpower around the world, with many students who took the test soon to enter into the tertiary system, then one might expect to see China's tertiary excellence gain traction. The EU is likely to show a large divergence in the quality of university freshmen in the region, and the US might lose its hegemony in terms of providing 'premium' tertiary education.

This report does not analyse data from the Programme for the International Assessment of Adult Competencies (PIAAC), which is also administered by the OECD, because tertiary education systems around the world have evolved so quickly in the past decade. The numeracy and literacy of the ca. 166,000 adults aged 16 to 65 who were surveyed do not reflect current trends in the quality and quantity of educational institutions, because these have evolved significantly since the majority of this cohort were at school.

Figure 8. Comparison of PISA results, 2012

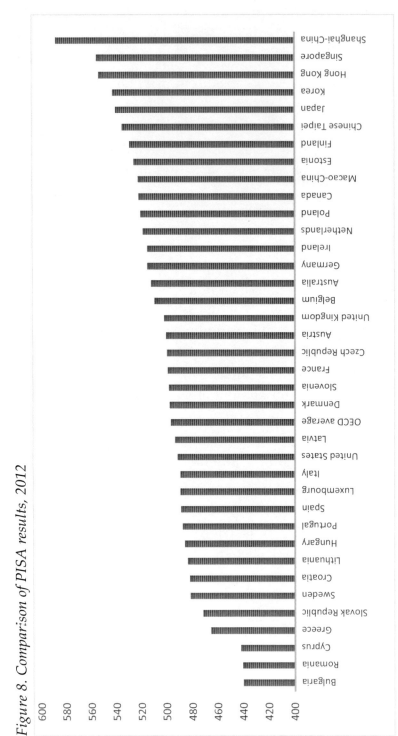

Notes: The scores presented here are a composite of the PISA subject results (three subject country scores combined and divided by three).

Source: Authors' configuration based on data from OECD (2013a).

What PIAAC can tell us about the current stock of human capital around the world (by comparing younger to older cohorts per country) is that education levels have improved in some countries more rapidly than in others, as younger cohorts vastly outperform older ones, Korea being an example of this. Other countries' skill proficiency remains relatively constant across generations, such as the UK or the US: "Young people in these countries are entering a much more demanding labour market, yet they are not much better prepared than those who are retiring" (OECD, 2013b). PIAAC also demonstrates that the quality of education varies widely, for example a tertiary education in one country can equate to the literacy skill level of a high school graduate in another: "Japanese and Dutch 25- to 34-year-olds who have only completed high school easily outperform some countries' university graduates of the same age" (OECD, 2013b).

Recommendation

Benchmark tertiary-educated persons around the globe.

Although the OECD's AHELO project has met considerable challenges, assessing what university students know at the end of their undergraduate studies would be an important way to better understand the quality of human capital around the globe. Such a project might best be piloted regionally (to overcome the challenges of globally diverse learning and testing cultures) and could be developed in cooperation with at least one non-regional partner (such as the US or Canada). Once the feasibility of the tertiary knowledge evaluation is established, further regional pilots could be initiated and methods for comparing skill levels inter-regionally could be developed. Such a tool should evaluate generic skills, but it could be expanded to examine discipline-specific skills. In the EU, the European Commission could consider fostering such an initiative.

3. PRIVATE AND PUBLIC FUNDING OF HIGHER EDUCATION IN THE EU, THE US AND CHINA

This chapter looks at both public and private funding of tertiary education using the following indicators:

- private and public expenditure on tertiary educational institutions as a percentage of GDP in 2010,
- annual expenditure per student by tertiary educational institutions for core services, ancillary services and R&D in 2010 and
- expenditure on research and development in China, 2009-13.

Because comparative data on spending efficiency are very limited, this section will only touch on this subject, but we would like to highlight the matter as an important factor in improving the quantity and quality of education. 'Smart spending' on higher education will be unique to each context. Smart spending measures could be broadly developed and could include both the public and private sectors working with universities to set targets and create incentives for the efficient use of higher education and research funding.

The US has outspent the EU and China on higher education for decades. In 2010, there was a large gap in funding for tertiary educational institutions between the EU and US. This gap was apparent both in funding as a percentage of GDP and in spending per student, with the US investing substantially more. The funding gap between the US and EU is primarily a result of large-scale private spending on tertiary education (including from tuition fees) in the US. There is, however, a wide variation in tertiary-education investment across the EU.

China's higher-education sector has been growing and consists of approximately 2,500 institutions (Ministry of Education of the People's Republic of China, 2013). It has recently set out to become an 'education nation', although it is a latecomer in the 'brain race'. One might think of this brain race as a version of the classic Aesop fable of "The Tortoise and the Hare". In this alternative narrative, however, the slower-moving tortoise begins with what it perceives to be a sufficient head start to win the race, but a late-coming hare then employs its speed and determination to win the race. This metaphor describes China's formula for success: make rapid gains and pursue clear goals, to counteract the disadvantages of entering the race late. With economic growth driving its progress, it is only a matter of time before China becomes a nation rich in human capital.

China's National Plan for Medium- and Long-Term Education Reform and Development (2010 to 2020), "sets a series of concrete goals to be achieved by 2020, including universalizing preschool education, improving nine-year compulsory education, raising the senior high school gross enrolment rate to 90 percent, and increasing the higher education gross enrolment rate to 40 percent" (Ministry of Education of the People's Republic of China, 2013). The 2010 Chinese Reform Plan in education also "promote[s] the separation of administrative and school operational functions" (Ministry of Education of the People's Republic of China, 2013). Increasing expenditure is one way in which the government aims to achieve these goals. And although some private money has been put into tertiary education, such investment is heavily regulated. Therefore, this sector is dominated by government spending (Ministry of Education of the People's Republic of China, 2013).

What data are available suggest that spending on tertiary education in China has on average lagged behind that in the US and the EU. But part of the 2010 Reform Plan in education is "increasing the government funding of education [at all levels] to 4 percent of GDP by 2012" (Wang,

2010), which the government declared it accomplished in December 2012. So although comparative data are scarce, we can assume that since 2010, investment in education has risen sharply; it had already been increasing in the prior decade. IMF data project that the Chinese economy will become the world's largest economy by the end of 2014 (Economist, 2014), so one can expect that both the levels of investment and the quantity and the quality of education in China will rise sharply in the coming years. China is also likely to succeed in attracting increasing numbers of its diaspora talent pool. Measures to prevent brain drain have been put in place for the return of skilled Chinese nationals.

Already, education policies and investments over the past decade in China have resulted in the 'massification' (expansion) of higher education and the establishment of a group of elite, world-class tertiary institutions. The government has launched several initiatives to accomplish this, two of which are dubbed 'Project 985' and 'Project 211' (Wang, 2010). Established in 1998, the Chinese government devoted funding to a 'Chinese Ivy League' of 39 universities through Project 985. Project 211, established in 1990, similarly aimed to develop around 100 institutions into world-class institutions. Regarding 'massification', as in the US and EU, getting into college or obtaining an undergraduate degree is no longer an extraordinary achievement in China. Undergraduate degrees all around the world are becoming but a single milestone on a longer journey to joining the emerging 'global talent class'. This is the segment of skilled persons who can effectively compete for high-paying jobs that require scarce skills outside of their own context and networks based on their exceptional achievement, or rare abilities.

As undergraduate education becomes the new norm for the middle classes, it is also becoming a prerequisite to running service-oriented and knowledge-based economies. The EU should therefore provide undergraduate education for a growing percentage (beyond its 40% target) of its population in the coming decades. Beyond this, the EU must also invest more heavily in attracting international persons with valuable skills, who are likely to boost economic and social innovation. This will require increasing both public and private investment in tertiary education in the EU, particularly in those EU countries that lag behind.

Many EU member states have been hit by austerity measures for a number of years. These measures have led to reductions in public investment, including in education, in many European countries, especially when measured as the relative share of total public expenditure (Van Damme, 2013). For example in 2011-12, "cuts [in education budgets] of more than 5% were observed in Greece, Italy, Hungary, Portugal and the United Kingdom (Wales), whereas decreases of between 1% and 5% were seen in Belgium (French Community), the Czech Republic, Estonia, France, Ireland, Poland, the Slovak Republic, Slovenia, Spain and the United Kingdom (Scotland)" (OECD, 2013c). Conversely, some EU countries were able to increase their educational budgets (in real terms) in the same period, namely Austria, Finland, Ireland and Luxembourg. The global economic crisis and its aftermath are likely to reinforce the differences in educational investment, including tertiary investment, across the EU for a long time to come.

The US has also been stricken by the economic ills of slow growth, including the inability of families and students to invest private money in tertiary education through tuition fees. China, however, has been able to sustain large-scale public investment. The following sections will look at these investment levels in more detail.

3.1 Public and private expenditure on tertiary educational institutions as a percent of GDP

Whereas comparative data on private and public expenditure on tertiary education are available for the EU and US, equivalent data for China are not reported in the standard OECD and UNESCO data sets. According to the OECD, in 2010 "expenditure on tertiary education amount[ed] to more than 1.5 percent of GDP in more than half of all [OECD] countries, and exceed[ed] 2.5 percent in Canada (2.7 percent), Korea (2.6 percent) and the United States (2.8 percent). Three countries devote[d] less than 1 percent of GDP to tertiary education, namely Brazil (0.9 percent), Hungary (0.8 percent) and the Slovak Republic (0.9 percent)" (OECD, 2013c). On average, the US spent significantly more as a percent of its GDP on its tertiary education institutions than the EU in 2010. The US spent on average 2.8% of its GDP on tertiary educational institutions, while the EU spent an average of 1.3% (Eurostat, 2014b).[7]

According to the Chinese government, "expenditures on research and development activities (R&D) was worth 1,190.6 billion Yuan in 2013 [approximately 190.5 billion USD], up 15.6 percent over 2012, accounting for 2.09 percent of GDP" (National Bureau of Statistics China, 2014). And in 2012, the Chinese government reported that "expenditures by universities amounted to 78.06 billion Yuan [approximately 12.5 billion USD]" (National Bureau of Statistics China, 2013). At the end of 2012, the government had invested 4% of GDP in education (all levels) (Wang, 2010).

Across the OECD, the public sector is the main pillar that supports tertiary education. Between 2000 and 2010, "84 percent of all funds for educational institutions come directly from public sources; 16 percent come from private sources" (OECD, 2013c). In the US, private-sector investment in higher education in the US has made a big difference on total tertiary education spending in 2010 (as it did in past decades). If public spending were taken into account, the US would spend at levels (as a percentage of GDP) similar to Mexico or Slovenia. Within the EU spending on tertiary education has varied significantly among countries, both in terms of its share of GDP and in terms of its private or public origin. Interestingly, increases in public and private expenditure have occurred simultaneously: "many of the OECD countries with the greatest growth in private spending have also had the largest increases in public funding" (OECD, 2013c).

---

[7] Data were not available for Belgium, Croatia or the Slovak Republic.

Figure 9. *Private and public expenditure on tertiary educational institutions as a percentage of GDP, 2010*

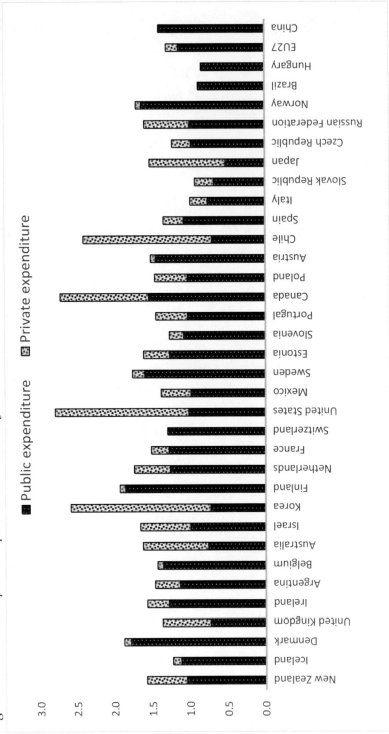

Sources: Authors' configuration based on data from OECD (2013c), Eurostat (2014b) and National Bureau of Statistics of China (2013).

Money by itself is not enough to guarantee high academic standards or a high place in university rankings. For example, the UK 'under-spends' both publically and privately in OECD comparison, but is the strongest EU country represented in global university-wide rankings – although it has to be noted that being located in an English-speaking country tends to elevate the ranking since most journals publish in English.

Increases in private funding of tertiary education have not produced a crowding-out effect on public spending in OECD countries in recent years: "The increase in private expenditure was not tied to a decrease in public spending on education. Rather, both sources of education expenditure had different growth rates" (OECD, 2013b). Additionally, the OECD found that: "At the country level, a higher share of private expenditure for tertiary education institutions is not associated with more limited access to tertiary education or decreasing opportunities for students from disadvantaged families to enrol in tertiary education" (OECD, 2013b). This evidence suggests that private funding is an important complement to public funding and should be encouraged more strongly throughout the EU.

The main components of private expenditure on higher education are investments from businesses (such as in research projects) and tuition and other student fees, although the share of each varies greatly. In Denmark, Finland and Germany, such contributions are non-existent or negligible. In the United Kingdom tuition and student fees make up more than 50% of the university budget. In Korea universities rely on tuition and student fees for more than 70% of their budgets (OECD, 2013c). Some universities in the US are renowned for their high tuition fees, but on average the share of tuition depends mainly on the type of institution. Tuition and student fees make up only 19% of American public university budgets; such contributions make up on average 29% of the budgets of private non-profit educational institutions (National Center for Education Statistics, 2013).

Generally, those countries that demand high tuition and fees also provide better access to loans, grants and scholarships, thus reducing the negative selection impact of such mandatory payments (OECD, 2013c). The pros and cons of tuition and student fees are highly debated among academics, administrators, policy-makers, students and the public. There is no 'one size fits all' model for best practice on this issue.

3.2   Public and private expenditure on tertiary educational institutions per student

This section compares the public and private expenditure per student in the EU, the US and China. Again, comparative OECD and UNESCO data for China are not available, but related national data will be used in order to understand funding trends in this area in China.

The US invests the most per student among OECD countries, spending around $18,000 on core student services in higher education. It also foots the largest bill per student for total tertiary spending by educational institution, which encompasses: core educational services, ancillary services (transport, housing, etc.) and R&D. In terms of total tertiary spending per student, Canada, Switzerland and Sweden take second, third and fourth place among OECD countries, spending $22,475, $21,893 and $19,562, respectively (OECD, 2013c). Again the EU institutions show a wide variation in per student. In the same spending category, Estonia spends only $6,501 and the Slovak Republic spends $6,904, (OECD, 2013c).

The following figure shows annual expenditure per student by tertiary educational institutions for core services, ancillary services and R&D.

Figure 10. Annual expenditure per student by tertiary educational institutions for core services, ancillary services and R&D, 2010

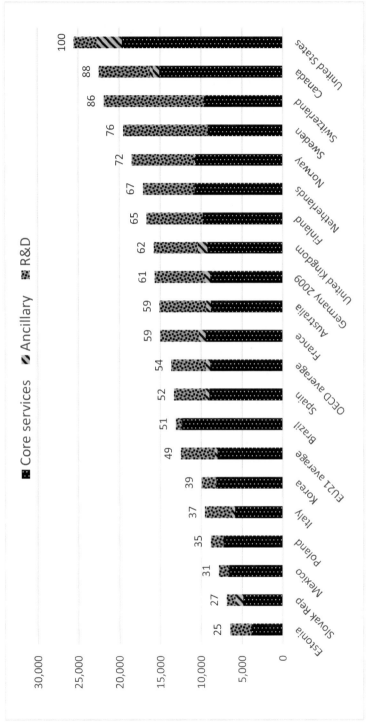

Sources: Authors' configuration based on data from OECD (2012b) and OECD (2013c).

China's investments in R&D have been increasingly substantially in recent years. In terms of spending in real terms, China ranked second in the world in 2011-12 (Battelle, 2011). The US was in first place, Japan placed third and Germany ranked fourth worldwide. According to the government, of its 1,190 billion Yuan R&D budget in 2013, "56.9 billion Yuan [$9.1 billion] was appropriated for fundamental research programs. A total number of 3,543 projects under the National Key Technology Research and Development Program and 2,118 projects under the Hi-tech Research and Development Program (the 863 Program) were implemented" (National Bureau of Statistics China, 2014).

China also saw a rise in the number of patent applications and progress in its space programme. Inspections and improvements in product quality were part of its R&D agenda. Although these data are not comparable to data available for the US and EU, the general trends indicate that the country is sharply increasing year-on-year investment in R&D (over 100% from 2009 to 2013) and is gaining ground fast on the spending-side of the tertiary education equation.

Figure 11. Expenditure on R&D activities in China, 2009-13

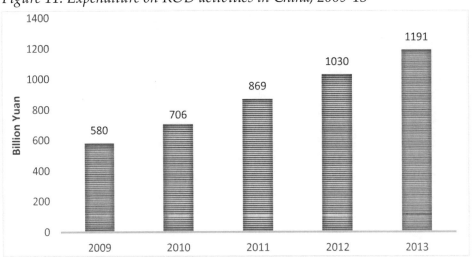

Source: Authors' configuration based on data from National Bureau of Statistics China (2014).

But is having the most expensive research programmes and students in the world a good thing? Methods of assessing the correlation between spending on tertiary education and education outcomes at that level are rudimentary at best, not least because there is no accurate international measure for comparative student performance at the tertiary level. One could, for example, correlate public spending as a proportion of gross domestic product (GDP) with one of the world university ranking outcomes (Juno, 2011). One such correlation was done by the QS intelligence unit, which publishes the QS Global University Ranking. It "used the higher education finance indicators provided by UNESCO, establishing four range groups (or quartiles) of public spending on tertiary education as a proportion of Gross Domestic Product (GDP) of the countries" (Juno, 2011). The outcome of this exercise was that for the time period 2000 to 2010, "university quality is not necessarily correlated with the proportion of public funding sources" (Juno, 2011).

Evidence also suggests that even in strongly privately funded systems, having fewer personal funds does not generally hinder access to tertiary education, as scholarship programmes shift burdens from families. And in the EU-21 a very different factor poses a barrier to access: social background. According to the OECD, "on average across EU-21 countries, a young person with at least one parent who has attained a tertiary degree is almost twice as likely (odds of 1.9) to be in higher education, compared to the proportion of such families in the population" (OECD, 2012c).

The OECD higher education correlates to better employment outcomes. For example, "the average employment rate for individuals with a tertiary-type A qualification was 88.0 percent for men and 81.1 percent for women" (OECD, 2012c) in the 21 EU member states for which comparative data was available in 2009. The economic crisis hit those with mid-range skills and jobs most severely. "Over the past decade, more than two-thirds of GDP growth in EU 21 countries was driven by labour income growth among tertiary-educated individuals, compared with just 51 percent in the United States" (OECD, 2012c). At a macro-level, demand for tertiary educated has continued to exceed supply in EU countries for which comparative data are available: "The relative earnings premium for those with a tertiary education increased in most EU 21 countries over the past ten years" (OECD, 2012c).

Recommendations

Increase support and spending-efficiency for higher education, without crowding out the public sector.

Funding tertiary education is a key responsibility of the state. While monitoring the impact of increased private support, the EU and its member states should create greater incentives for the private funding of education and increasingly profile best practice regarding spending efficiency by universities. This could be done through private-sector investments in R&D (to increase innovation), scholarships and internships (to increase access to learning) and programmes that help students make the transition from university to work (to find jobs that match their skills). Both the public and private sectors should work with universities to set targets and create incentives for the efficient use of higher education and research funding. For those institutions that set and meet 'smart spending targets', additional funding should be made available as part of an incentive system.

Foster a 'client-based' and co-knowledge-production learning culture at universities.

Learning cultures at universities can be very diverse, and too often students are not viewed as the universities' most important clients. Universities in the EU should find ways to become more service-oriented (such as increasing the academic advisory role of teachers and professors). They should also view students as co-producers of knowledge and should foster such a culture both inside and outside the classroom.

4. GAME-CHANGING FACTORS IN INNOVATING HIGHER EDUCATION

This chapter analyses three key factors that are shaping and will shape both the quantity and quality of education:

• technology and the digitalisation of education,
• education and employability and
• governance in higher education.

4.1 Technology and the digitalisation of education

The digitalisation of education is perhaps the largest and most unpredictable factor that is changing learning at all levels, including at the tertiary level. It will not only affect the way students learn, but it will transform how teachers teach and how the performance of students is monitored and assessed. For example, there have been improvements in our understanding of how students learn, which helps teachers to communicate better with students and to tailor their teaching methods to students' individual needs. This is expected to stop the rise of the cost of learning per student in the medium to long term, or even bring it down.

Technology, and in particular advances in digital technology, will challenge the very business models of many traditional brick-and-mortar institutions. It will most likely produce winners and losers in the education provision sector with some fully utilising the new technology to their advantage and others specialising in the classical model. Most institutions presumably will opt for blended learning – a mixture of both. Technological advances will open up a whole new world of options for learners and teachers. It also has the potential to prepare incoming workforces with a broad set of digital skills, which will allow them to quickly adapt to the constantly changing technological knowledge needed for tomorrow's jobs. These changes demand a proactive approach to understanding how digital education is changing learning.

The largest advances in digital education so far have been developed and launched in the US. The Massive Open Online Courses (MOOC) sector is currently dominated by three US providers: Coursera, edX and Udacity. China is a latecomer; it entered the MOOC market in 2013, when Peking and Tsinghua Universities made courses available via Coursera and edX. Tsinghua University also launched its own platform XuetangX. Kaikeba and TopU also offer MOOCs locally in China (Embassy of Switzerland in China, 2014). Chinese universities are caught between the potential advantages of bringing education to scale at a low cost and the danger of losing control over the ideas its young people are exposed to (Forestier, 2013). Chinese universities and education providers have invested in translating online learning material into Chinese, but they have not yet developed a clear digital education strategy. This could change quickly in the coming years, however, as China is the largest higher-education market in the world.

European higher-learning institutions have entered the digital education game with increasing vigour in the past two years. According to the European University Association (EUA), "around one-third of MOOCs around the world involve European higher education institutions" (Gaebel, 2014). A 2013 survey conducted by the EUA showed that open online courses are just beginning to attract the attention of European universities. For example, the EUA survey in the same year showed that over 40% of the 175 European university leaders questioned had never heard of a MOOC (Gaebel, 2013). However, nearly 90% of those surveyed expressed a desire to learn more about the topic. Those universities that specialised in degree-based distance learning, such as the UK's Open University, are perhaps the most advanced in Europe at strategically combining online and offline education.

OpenupEd is a pan-European initiative for open online courses, initiated by the European Association of Distance Teaching Universities

(EADTU). Launched in April 2013 by partners in 11 European countries, OpenupEd is expected to grow exponentially with much interest from institutions all over Europe (UpenupEd, 2014). Courses posted on the platform conform to a common framework featuring eight parameters, including credential recognition of successfully completed courses. OpenupEd is funded by the European Commission as part of its strategy to open up education through new technologies, which was launched in April 2013 (European Commission, 2014e). The EU Commission's Erasmus+ and Horizon 2020 programmes also offer funding that is increasingly being spent on digital learning. Furthermore, on 27 March 2014, the European Commission launched a network to foster web talent through Massive Open Online Courses (European Commission, 2014a).

At the national level in the EU, the most notable digital education platforms have been developed in the UK (Future Learn), Spain (Miriada X), France (Orange) and Germany (Iversity). At the university level the international consortium EUROTECH is noteworthy. The May 2014 Presidency discussion paper, "Education crossing borders: new opportunities and challenges", is continuing to advance both online and offline cooperation in education and training (Council of the European Union, 2014).

While much has happened in the last few years, the digital revolution in education is still only beginning. Initiatives that seem innovative today could be obsolete in a few years' time. This is characteristic of developing markets, especially in technology, as can be seen in the rise and recent fall of the smart phone company BlackBerry. So it is understandable that the European Commission and the majority of tertiary institutions in Europe have taken a wait-and-see approach to digital education and the changing mainstreamed (online-and-offline) business model that is quickly engulfing the education sector.

The European MOOCs scoreboard (European Commission, 2014b) is an instructive example of this approach to the use of new technology in education. The scoreboard tracks the number of such courses produced, or co-produced, by European learning institutions. As of April

2014, 510 MOOCs were on offer involving European institutions (in this case, Europe includes EU member states, as well as Switzerland, Norway, Turkey and Russia). Spain led the pack with 198 such courses, followed by the United Kingdom (92), France (63) and Germany (55). Countries whose learning institutions have created five or fewer MOOCs were: Lithuania (1), Slovakia (1), Norway (1), Ireland (2), Estonia (2), Portugal (2), Sweden (4) and Finland (5) (European Commission, 2014b). In contrast to the US, Europe is not home to a major concentration of digital education platforms. Europe's MOOCs market is decentralised. In addition, European universities, which are largely publicly-funded, are less attractive to commercial e-learning providers than the US market, which is richer with venture capital and private funding of higher education.

Yet the EU has one decisive advantage that has not yet become part of the broader political and public debate on its digital learning strategy: the European Credits System allows for the easy transfer of credits from one university to the other (Lisbon Recognition Convention) (Council of Europe, 1997). It places the burden of non-recognition on universities, so that if they cannot prove a significant difference in a student's accredited study, they must give official recognition to the student's academic achievement. So those select MOOCs that are developed and approved for credit at one university can be taken by students from any other European university. The credits earned can be put towards any student's degree. Albeit being difficult to implement in practice, the transferability of accredited academic achievement offers great potential for increasing the quantity and quality of education (and possibly decreasing the cost over time) and taking inter-university cooperation to a whole new level.

It is likely that universities will increasingly enable learning by offering students a selection of international 'learning bundles', partially online and partially offline. This will inevitably change the business models of higher education institutions, as some of the learning bundles will be free online courses, and some will involve classroom learning and face-to-face collaboration with other students. One could foresee universities adopting a model for earning a degree at their institution that required a minimum number of on-campus offline learning experiences, as well as online learning that is home-made by the student's institution.

One could also envisage that students might sign up for a personalised degree by picking and choosing courses from a number of universities and 'contracting' one institution to monitor and accredit their achievement. In this second model the student might take very few courses from the accrediting institution and, in case tuition fees are charged at all, might face a different (lower) price tag than he or she would at universities requiring a minimum load of on-campus studies.

Indeed one might see the divide between teaching and accrediting grow as higher education becomes more diverse and individualised. It is imaginable that accrediting 'higher education bundles' could become an industry in its own right. It may also emerge that personalising online courses becomes a niche business in the higher education sector. For example, a formerly massive open online course by a renowned academic would be expanded and taught as a personalised open online course (POOC) in an adaptive environment suited to individual learning goals, needs, pace and style. Not least, collaborating with renowned professors and providing high-quality online courses may prove to be a tool for improving the international reputation of European universities.

Recommendations

Support and more closely monitor advances in digital learning.

The EU and its member states should support and monitor the digital learning initiatives of European institutions of higher education more strongly. Universities should summarise their digital learning activities as part of their standard institutional profile.

Take advantage of cross-institutional learning in the digital age.

The European Credits System allows for the easy transfer of credits from one university to the other. The EU and its member states should use its credit transferability advantage more strategically. Universities should examine how on- and offline learning models could be integrated to improve the quality and quantity of education. Public and private funding incentives in the EU and its member states should be examined to enable universities that have developed digital strategies to pursue these in greater scope.

4.2 Education and employability

This section looks at policies that attract and retain international students, at job-matching initiatives and at how universities are increasingly taking into account the employability of their graduates. It will:

- outline the contours of a shifting global economic balance,
- explore shifts in talent flows,
- analyse demographic shifts and corresponding labour shortage forecasts and
- look at policy trends that encourage student mobility and match skills with employment.

The global economic landscape will change drastically over the coming decades. China is changing the post-war global economic world order. The IMF's economic forecasts suggest that by the end of 2014 China will have become the biggest economy (in purchasing power parity – or PPP) in the world. With a recalibrated global economic balance, talent flows are likely to shift towards growing economies, where employment opportunities are more plentiful. Since the mid-1970s the number of international students worldwide has quadrupled. In 2011, 4.3 million students studied abroad (OECD, 2013c). Trends concerning where international students come from and where they go have been changing in the past decade. From 2000 to 2011, the percentage of foreign tertiary students that go to the US and Germany has decreased, but these countries – along with the UK, France, Australia and Canada – remain the most popular destinations for international students.

The international students that make up the globally mobile talent pool increasingly come from Asia. The largest cohort in 2011 was from China (723,000 students), followed by India (223,000 students). Korean students (139,000) were the third most internationally mobile group, followed by German students (132,000) and Turkish students (83,000) (OECD, 2011b). Language and tuition fees play a role, as also does immigration policy, in the choice of destination. University reputation is another important element influencing students' choice of destination.

China is an increasingly attractive destination for international exchange students and is expected to become even more attractive in the coming years. Chinese students are the largest single cohort of international students worldwide; where they go indicates in large part which destinations are the most competitive. According to the projections in the China's 12th Five-Year Plan (2011-15), "the Chinese government will support about 50,000 international students in China in 2015", and the country will become the largest Asian destination for such students in 2020. Du Yubo, Vice-Minister of Education, said that by 2020, "about 500,000 international students will be in China, enabling the country to become the largest Asian destination for international students" (Chinese Scholarship Council, 2013).

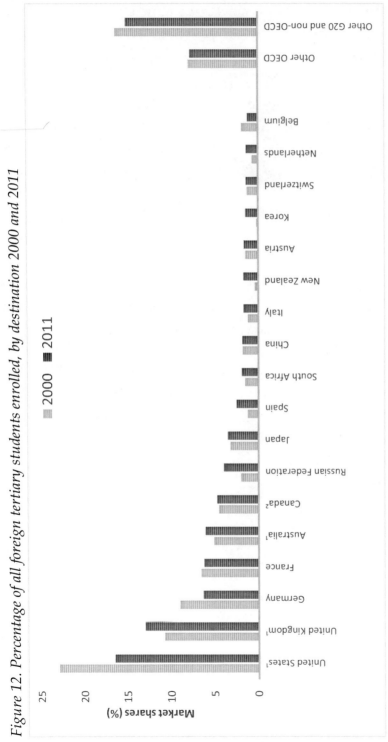

Figure 12. Percentage of all foreign tertiary students enrolled, by destination 2000 and 2011

Note: Year of reference of data for countries other than OECD and G20 is 2010 instead of 2011.

[1] Data relate to international students defined on the basis of their country of residence. Data for the UK for 2011 are based on citizenship.

Source: Authors' configuration based on data from OECD (2013c).

Figure 13. Percentage of foreign tertiary students enrolled worldwide, by region of origin, 2011

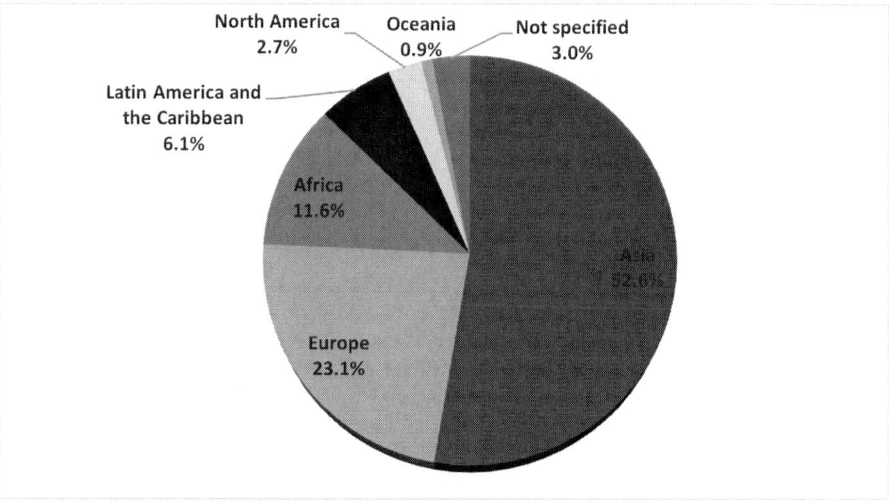

Source: Authors' configuration based on data from OECD (2013c).

Although annual growth in China has been slowing, the country achieved a real growth rate of over 7% in 2012, which it is expected to maintain over the coming years. Such a growth rate is currently out of reach for Europe and the US. China is a demographic billionaire, yet this demographically wealthy country has a declining working population, because of its long-standing one-child policy, which has transformed the country's demographic development dramatically since 1979 (although the policy has been relaxed, most recently in 2013).

Between 2010 and 2050, the Chinese labour force is expected to shrink by nearly 20% (KKR Insights, 2012). A contracting work force could jeopardise future economic growth in the country. Thus, China is expected to increasingly 'fish' in the global talent pool to attract skilled workers from abroad when gaps emerge in its own labour market. With rising salaries and its capacity to invest in R&D,[8] China's attractiveness to international graduates is likely to increase.

---

[8] In 2012, total R&D investment in China reached 1 trillion Yuan at a high growth rate – above 15% annually – which shows no sign of slowing down.

The World Economic Forum's 2013-2014 Global Competitiveness Index includes the indicator "country capacity to attract talent". According to this indicator, the United Kingdom was the fourth and Germany was the 20th most-capable country in terms of attracting talent from abroad (World Economic Forum, 2014). These two countries scored the highest of the large EU countries. Smaller EU member states, such as Luxembourg, Ireland, Malta, the Netherlands and Sweden, came ahead of China. China was 26th worldwide in its capacity to attract talent (World Economic Forum, 2014).

Europe's working-age population is declining and labour shortages are predicted to become more pronounced across the EU. Both the EU and China are therefore expected to fish in the talent pool, increasingly and simultaneously, in the coming decades. Two large European economies, namely Poland and Germany, are already experiencing a decline in their labour forces, whereas all EU countries with the exception of the UK and Sweden will face the same challenge during the next decade. Shortages will be spread unevenly across professions, but labour shortages will occur in many high-skilled occupations (McKinsey Global Institute, 2012a).

With EU directives on the Blue Card, posted workers, seasonal workers, easing conditions of admission for students (Council of the European Union, 2004) and the admission of researchers from third countries (Council of the European Union, 2005), the EU has made progress toward creating standards for admittance, labour market access and intra-EU mobility policies for non-EU citizens. The Council's directive on admission of researchers in particular can be viewed as guidance for further thinking on EU mobility of talent. In accordance with this Directive 2004/114/EC, students from outside of the EU arc allowed, under certain conditions, to pursue studies in member states as long as their visa does not expire. However after graduation, opportunities to remain and seek employment depend on national regulations in each member state.

Figure 14. Labour supply forecast by regions and countries, 2012-20 and 2020-30

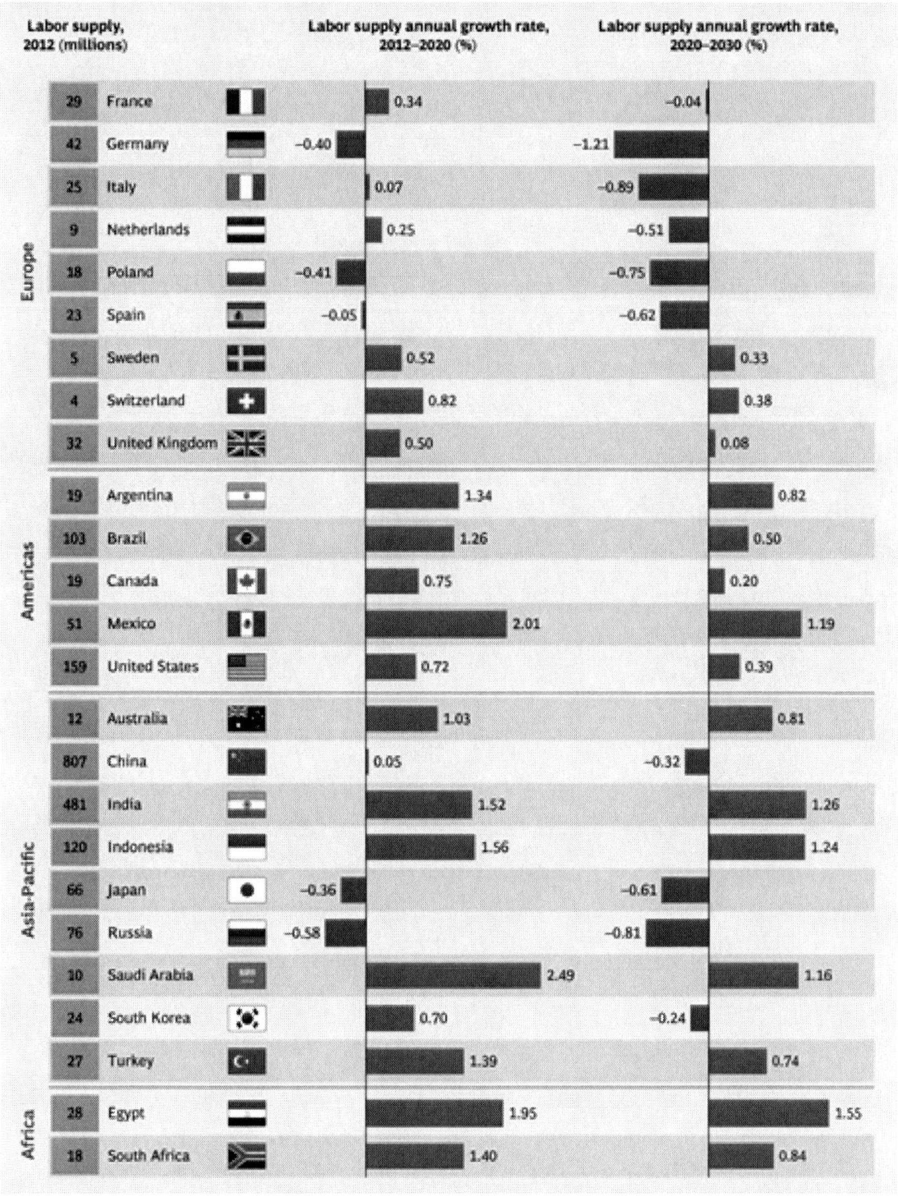

		Labor supply, 2012 (millions)	Labor supply annual growth rate, 2012–2020 (%)	Labor supply annual growth rate, 2020–2030 (%)
Europe	France	29	0.34	−0.04
	Germany	42	−0.40	−1.21
	Italy	25	0.07	−0.89
	Netherlands	9	0.25	−0.51
	Poland	18	−0.41	−0.75
	Spain	23	−0.05	−0.62
	Sweden	5	0.52	0.33
	Switzerland	4	0.82	0.38
	United Kingdom	32	0.50	0.08
Americas	Argentina	19	1.34	0.82
	Brazil	103	1.26	0.50
	Canada	19	0.75	0.20
	Mexico	51	2.01	1.19
	United States	159	0.72	0.39
Asia-Pacific	Australia	12	1.03	0.81
	China	807	0.05	−0.32
	India	481	1.52	1.26
	Indonesia	120	1.56	1.24
	Japan	66	−0.36	−0.61
	Russia	76	−0.58	−0.81
	Saudi Arabia	10	2.49	1.16
	South Korea	24	0.70	−0.24
	Turkey	27	1.39	0.74
Africa	Egypt	28	1.95	1.55
	South Africa	18	1.40	0.84

Note: Figures for 2020 and 2030 assume the same participation rate by sex and age groups. The labour supply is the forecast of the total population (age 15 and over, divided into five-year age groups) times the labour force participation rate (per five-year age group).

Source: Boston Consulting Group (2013), based on UN Population Division database; ILO LABORSTA database.

Allowing for increased mobility and access to employment opportunities for recent graduates from EU universities is one area in which the EU could improve its attractiveness to foreign talent. The EU could, for example, set up a set period for recent graduates to find work within the EU without having to go through additional visa and work permit procedures. Several member states have already created national policies that allow non-EU citizens to remain in the country to find a job after graduation. Germany is currently becoming one of the most open countries when it comes to the admission of third-country nationals and in providing incentives to retain highly skilled workers. In 2005 Germany reformed its *Zuwanderungsgesetz* (immigration law), opening its economy to further immigration of skilled labour. Since August 2012, another amendment has been passed that grants students up to 18 months after graduation to find a job in Germany, thus extending the visa for this period (Auswertiges Amt, 2012). This offer may attract future students and could boost Germany's talent competitiveness.

The German government has realised that demographic trends will prevent labour demand from being met by domestic labour supply. Labour shortages were already becoming more pronounced after the financial crisis when German unemployment rates dropped to a 10-year low. In 2012, immigration to Germany was second only to immigration to the US and its policies to attract foreign talent are bearing fruit (OECD, 2014). While in 2012 most newspapers featured stories of insufficient migration or labour mobility to Germany, recent stories claim there is too much. The word 'welfare tourism' is receiving more attention although recent studies find that Romanians and Bulgarians (who are portrayed in the media as the worst exploiters of German social benefits) are actually net contributors to the economy (Brücker et al., 2012).

Even if the unemployment rate of recent immigrants tends to be higher than for German citizens, those who do find a job quickly compensate, and more, for any perceived drain on the economy. This is particularly true for immigrants with tertiary-level education, since their income is on average higher, yielding higher tax revenues. Furthermore, assuming that immigrants are relatively young, as recent university graduates often are, the need for healthcare provision is small and their contributions to the pension system are vital for its sustainability, at least for pay-as-you-go systems. Overall, it can be expected that Germany will profit from the fostered immigration of skilled labour, although excessive, oversimplified and generalised discussions on welfare tourism may limit the appetite of policy-makers to address migration reforms that could improve the EU's competitiveness.

Of course individual member states could pursue national migration reforms for non-EU graduates in the absence of an EU directive. From the perspective of non-EU students, however, limiting job opportunities to one country after graduation reduces the attractiveness of this country as a potential study destination. For example, offering a student from Shanghai (which has a population of more than 24 million people, making this city larger than the majority of EU member states) only the possibility of residing and working in a country of just six million people for a number of years may seem like an unacceptable limitation. Increasingly, the scale and flexibility of opportunities are likely to play a role in the competitiveness of EU member states. From a European perspective it is far better if graduates look for job opportunities in those countries in the EU that have the highest need for their skills. Of course a non-bureaucratic procedure for finding employment for recent non-EU graduates would increase the probability of successfully matching demand and supply for qualified job-seekers in the EU. Providing recent graduates with the opportunity to move within Europe to find a job would not only improve the chances of a vacancy being filled, but it would be a way to attract students as well.

Such a policy could also help distribute talent across EU member states more evenly. For example, a student might opt to study in a location in the EU periphery if he or she can then seek a job across the EU upon graduation. This would have both advantages and disadvantages. The talent balance between member states might tip in favour of emerging talent hubs within the EU. On the other hand, since a scheme like this might attract new talent to more obscure locations, it could lead to the emergence of new 'talent hubs' in places that might not otherwise develop them. In order to foster EU competitiveness, the EU could introduce a 'Graduate Mobility Card', which would entitle recent graduates to move freely across the EU within a restricted period (say, e.g. 6-12 months) to seek a job. The impact of opening the intra-EU labour market to recent graduates would be gradual but ultimately self-energising.

Initiatives to foster the matching of labour supply and demand in Europe could bridge skill gaps and improve the economic competitiveness of the EU. Governments, universities and the private sector might raise awareness among students about professions that are expected to demand skilled workers. The accurate prediction of labour supply and demand and the use of this information (by governments, universities and the private sector) to counsel students, will become an important element in determining the competitiveness of continents whose working population is in decline.

China is currently looking at internal migration policies as a way to improve job- and skills-matching. Since the 1990s and 2000s, the Hukou[9] system of controlled internal migration in China has been steadily eased and in 2013 Premier Jiabao announced that the government intends to introduce a system of residency permits and abolish the old Hukou system. Consequently, government restrictions on internal labour mobility limit the ability of the market to foster skills and job-matching. However, even if Chinese graduates were completely mobile, the draw of China's megacities could lead to the abandonment of other areas. The phenomenon of 'moving east' to coastal regions is increasingly appealing to young graduates and has contributed to a widening talent gap in the west of China.

---

[9] The Hukou system is a registry of households with all its family members. Moving to another region requires a permit, which is difficult to acquire. The Hukou system prevents a massive outflow from rural areas of China to the more prosperous cities.

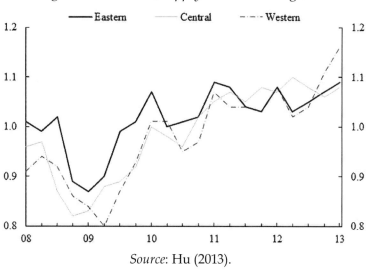

Figure 15. Demand/supply ratio across regions

Source: Hu (2013).

At the end of 2013, the Chinese Ministry of Human Resources and Social Security estimated job vacancies at 6 million. According to the IMF, China's unemployment rate is 4.1% of a labour force estimated at 815 million, which equals 33 million persons unemployed (Gros & Alcidi, 2013). Thus the matching performance is marginally better than in the EU.

China is expected to suffer from a supply deficit of eight million graduates by 2020 (McKinsey, 2013). Over the next ten years it will become increasingly important to find ways to match a highly skilled work force to appropriate jobs. Because of its aging workforce, China (like the EU) has to employ its human capital more carefully. Government intervention in fostering STEM skills may help balance the country's changing labour needs. In 2010, almost 50% of Chinese graduates earned a bachelor degree in science or engineering, whereas this figure was 35% in the EU (National Science Board, 2014). However, the quality of graduates from Chinese universities may pose a problem for Chinese competitiveness. McKinsey estimates that only one out of 10 Chinese-educated engineers is capable of working in an international corporation in their field.

In the US, the government is not much involved in matching graduates to jobs. Job and skill matches are facilitated primarily by the market and universities' cooperation with businesses. The EU has recently invested significant resources in job-matching. The flagship initiative of the European Commission is the European Employment Services (EURES), which connects national employment agencies with social partners and advertises vacancies across Europe on its website. Employers upload their vacancies specifying the skills required, remuneration, type of contract and other information that enables EURES to match them with the uploaded CVs of jobseekers. The CVs are digital and acquired qualifications can be selected from a dropdown menu, hence increasing the potential of an algorithmic matching process. Job-seekers can forward their applications to jobs listed on EURES and likewise employers can contact suitable candidates directly. In their search, job-seekers can select vacancies by occupation as well as by country or even regions they would be willing to work in. Additionally, the EURES portal allows users to download their CVs in the standardised Europass format.

To overcome language barriers, the website is available in all 25 EEA languages and new steps are being taken to improve user-friendliness. There are approximately 1.5 million vacancies currently listed on EURES and nearly 30,000 recently maintained CVs have been uploaded. Given the size of the European labour market, EURES covers a small portion of the employment market. The European Skills/Competences, qualifications and Occupation (ESCO) project launched by the European Commission aims to further improve the recognition of skills by setting a common language framework for work titles and qualifications. The successful implementation of ESCO, once it is finalised, should significantly boost job- and skills-matching across Europe, especially for job-seekers with vocational training. This leaves much scope for better skills-matching within Europe for the benefit of the individual as well as the economy as a whole. By the end of 2013, over 2.2 million job vacancies had been registered in the industry, construction and services sectors alone and this figure does not include Italy, France, Ireland, Denmark or Malta (Eurostat, 2014). [10] After adding those countries and the agricultural sector into the calculations, it can be assumed that there are more than three million vacancies across the EU. Over a million job vacancies alone are registered in Germany. At the same time, over 26 million persons in the EU are looking for a job (Ameco, 2014).

In the coming decades, a population's employability, and particularly that of its highly skilled members, will be of increasing importance to its well-being, and to the development of robust economies. Awareness of this importance has been growing among universities. For example, the Aalto University in Helsinki merged several smaller universities into one and linked its university closely to local businesses. Aalto University receives donations from private corporations and creates joint research and study opportunities with companies. This broad-ranging collaboration is designed to achieve breakthroughs in research and development that will help companies innovate (Aalto University, 2014). These links benefit not only the university but also the student. Students gain insights into the labour market and build networks.

Universities have realised that practical experience during study is highly valued by corporations and so they offer the students the possibility of internships. However, not all universities have understood the value of linking studies with internships. A flexible curriculum and the offer of academic credit for relevant internships would improve the employability of graduates.

The university ranking system recently developed by Quacquarelli Symonds identifies which aspects of a university most attract students (QS, 2014a and b). Their student survey found that employment prospects upon graduation are one of students' most important criteria when choosing a university. Therefore QS places strong emphasis on

---

[10] No consistent data are available for these countries.

employability in their rankings and they are not the only ones. The Global Employability University ranking published by the International Herald Tribune is a table based on a survey of 2,700 recruiters in 20 different countries, which focuses on the employability associated with different universities (Times Higher Education, 2014a). One way in which universities might better gauge their own performance and policy-makers could get information for improving skills-matching is through tracking the careers of their alumni. Information about graduates' careers could be included as an indicator for measuring employability as part of a university's performance.

Recommendations

Improve the mobility of non-EU graduates.

The EU as a whole is more attractive to international students than any one of its member states is on its own. The EU should help European universities increase their appeal to non-EU students by introducing a Graduate Mobility Card, which would allow non-EU citizens who graduate from EU universities to look for employment in all EU member states for a period of time following the completion of their European degree.

Improve job and skills matching.

With an increasing proportion of the global population completing tertiary degrees, skills- and job-matching for graduates with appropriate jobs is becoming important to maintaining healthy economies. Market forces alone do not adequately match qualifications with employment opportunities. Students should be better informed about how their educational choices relate to employment through the incorporation of employability indicators in university rankings. Additionally, public and commercial skills and job-matching initiatives should be developed to create low-cost and efficient information portals that match employers with the talent they seek.

Use the knowledge and experiences of university alumni better.

Universities should keep better track of the experiences of their alumni and make special effort to solicit their insights regarding looking for work. Building and maintaining alumni networks can benefit universities in many ways, and these networks can foster job-matching and help university leaders understand how well their curricula prepare students to enter the labour market.

4.3   Governance in higher education

Governance in higher education is a mixture of many elements, such as organisational architecture, faculty and student rights and obligations, and the acquisition and management of financial resources. At a minimum, good university governance includes:

- aligning the interests of a wide variety of stakeholders, both internal and external;
- permitting the university to perform to its strengths and to correct its weaknesses;
- balancing excellence with fair and transparent access to learning; and
- allowing universities to fill educational services within a landscape of competing institutions.

Good governance of higher education cannot be measured in absolute terms with a single indicator. Its parameters are strongly influenced by organisational architecture and the legal and policy frameworks in which universities are embedded. The idea of good governance also varies in relation to other similar or comparable institutions. Good governance can broadly be assessed on: learning outcomes, research outcomes, ability to attract excellent faculty, academic freedom, access to funding, etc. This section will only touch on a few important issues of university governance that apply (although differently) across an extremely diverse range of national and regional contexts. With the caveat that we are comparing 'apples and oranges' in this section, for which comparative data are not yet available, selected examples from the US, China and EU will be examined to broadly establish some relative strengths and weaknesses.[11]

China has one of the most regulated and bureaucratic university governance systems in the world. The reasons for this are both historical and multifaceted. They include a strong desire on the part of the government to influence teaching and a need for coherence within the system at a time of rapid expansion of tertiary education, heavy government investment and tremendous quality upgrades in higher education. As the country goes from being a manufacturing centre to a knowledge-based economy, education policies are becoming less top-down and more 'multidirectional'. The government sets targets, provides funding, is present in university administration and monitors progress to see that targets are met on time. The 'massification' of higher education across China and the setting up of several elite universities are two examples of how the government has used its highly bureaucratic all-embracing system of governance to make rapid progress towards the goals it sets for higher education.

Maintaining government control and coherency in the higher education system and ensuring that this education is relevant to the economy may prove to be difficult. Since 1992, the Chinese government has been working towards a more market-oriented economy (Downes, 2012). Higher education is part of China's National Innovation System (NIS), which has in turn caused shifts in the role of the state in university governance. The government has encouraged "greater cooperation between research institutes, the higher education system and enterprises" (Downes et al., 2012). The Chinese government aims to de-bureaucratise universities to improve their governance. More autonomy

---

[11] Four extensive reports on the governance of universities – Centre for Higher Education Policy Studies (2008), the European Commission (2008) and Estermann et al. (2011) – only provide data for Europe. Similarly Aghion et al. (2010) have two datasets, one for the European economies and one for the US. None of the studies contains data for China.

for universities was part of the 2010 National Plan for Medium- and Long-Term Education Reform and Development (Jiang, 2011).

Nevertheless, heavy local government involvement is characteristic of China's university governance. In general, universities are "administered at the provincial and/or central level. A unique characteristic of the Chinese system is the presence of a dual administrative structure, wherein the Chinese Communist Party sets up its own administrative structure within each university, parallel to the administrative system" (Varghese & Martin, 2013). This makes the tertiary education a by-design system, like a mosaic, where the various pieces give a bigger picture when viewed together.

Table 1. Chinese government involvement in university governance

Year	Total	Run by central gov't	Run by local gov't	Private HEIs
1995	1,054	358	696	-
2000	1,041	116	925	-
2005	1,792	111	1,431	250
2009	2,305	111	1,463	658

Source: Authors' own elaboration based on data from Min (2011).

China has recently introduced a system of 'presidential responsibility' which allows a good deal of autonomy to many universities (Varghese & Martin, 2013). China has a hard road ahead in terms of balancing what will become increasingly difficult trade-offs for the government. As at all universities around the world, the best students will not base themselves in China without globally-competitive standards of academic freedom, access to information and the ability to publish research results.

Since the governance of universities in the US has received more scrutiny and is therefore more familiar, it will only be touched upon briefly here. The American Association of University Professors (AAUP) is one of the oldest institutions to have addressed the question of improving university governance (American Association of University Professors, 2014). The Association grew out of the conviction widely held in the US that the rights of the faculty must be protected within governance structures. The US tertiary education system on average is run with a high degree of autonomy from the state. Broadly speaking, university autonomy in the US is seen as giving universities a comparative advantage over universities in other countries. Decisions regarding curricula, staffing, research, organisational architecture, etc. are made independently, which allows well-run institutions to excel at their strengths and to address their weaknesses.

Participatory governance including student and faculty contributions to improving governance allow for new ways of addressing problems. The US system, in contrast to more centralised university governance systems, can be thought of as a mosaic, in which each piece is coloured to its own advantage. When all the pieces are placed together, the big picture is less obvious. Market forces, as well as trial and error, create the dynamics of system-wide evolution, with low-demand educational services leaving the market and new niches and branches of education entering it. This evolution is less strategic, more fragmented and less policy-driven than in countries and regions that have a predominately publicly-funded tertiary system.

In the EU, the biggest issue in the area of reforming university governance is autonomy. The EUA, for example, has created a university autonomy scorecard (European University Institution, 2014). It looks at university governance under four headings: organisational, financial, staffing and academic autonomy (see Table 2).

The governance of higher education in the EU is an extremely complex matter, with seemingly all levels of government somehow involved across the various legal arrangements in the 28 member states. The EU also plays an important role in looking at all the pieces of the 'mosaic', through the so-called European Research Area (ERA). In very broad terms, the ERA aims to draw the efforts of European universities (and the governments that fund them) together in a more coherent 'big picture', driven by the idea that research does not stop at the borders of EU member states (Federal Ministry of Education and Research Germany 2014). For example, as noted by the European Commission (2014c), "the 2014 ERA Survey will be crucial for identifying areas where progress in the implementation of actions required to complete a single market for researchers, knowledge and technology has been made".

The EU adds a level of bureaucracy to university governance, but also adds value by increasing funding and combating the risk of a fragmented higher education sector, that duplicates work or misses important opportunities for synergy in innovation. The ERA is part of the Innovation Union initiative and Europe 2020 Strategy (Federal Ministry of Education and Research Germany, 2014). It builds on a large body of initiatives and policy frameworks. With it and related programmes, the EU cites the following qualities as being of particular importance:

- more effective national research systems (previously 'modern universities'),

- optimal transnational cooperation and competition (previously 'joint programming' and 'research infrastructure'),

- an open labour market for researchers (previously 'mobility and career development for researchers'),

- gender equality and gender mainstreaming in research (new priority) and

- optimal circulation, access to and transfer of scientific knowledge including via digital ERA (previously 'knowledge transfer / intellectual property') (Federal Ministry of Education and Research Germany, 2014).

Table 2. Criteria for the university autonomy scorecard

Organisational autonomy	Financial autonomy	Staffing autonomy	Academic autonomy
• Selection procedure for the executive head	• Length and type of public funding	• Capacity to decide on recruitment procedures (senior academic/senior administrative staff)	• Capacity to decide on overall student numbers
• Selection criteria for the executive head	• Ability to keep surplus	• Capacity to decide on salaries (senior academic/senior administrative staff)	• Capacity to select students (BA, MA)
• Dismissal of the executive head	• Ability to borrow money		• Capacity to introduce programmes (BA, MA)
• Term of office of the executive head	• Ability to own buildings	• Capacity to decide dismissals (senior academic/senior administrative staff)	• Capacity to terminate programmes
• Inclusion and selection of external members in governing bodies	• Ability to charge tuition fees for national/EU students (BA, MA, PhD)	• Capacity to decide on promotions (senior academic/senior administrative staff)	• Capacity to choose the language of instruction (BA, MA)
• Capacity to decide on academic structures	• Ability to charge tuition fees for non-EU students (BA, MA, PhD)		• Capacity to select quality assurance mechanisms and providers
• Capacity to create legal entities			• Capacity to design content of degree programmes

Source: Estermann et al. (2011).

The EU, the US and China represent very different kinds of higher education governance. There are large differences among the EU member states in particular, yet surprisingly the cases highlight some common issues. University governance is a means to an end. Drawing from the EUA's University Autonomy Scorecard (Estermann et al., 2011), one might envisage an extra-EU expansion and adaptation of this idea. Rather than using university autonomy as the basis for comparison, one might look at university governance and evaluate the following indicators:

- level of autonomy,

- university performance (academic freedom, student satisfaction),

- quality of education,

- income security and diversification,

- attractiveness to international staff and students (internationalisation, including internationalisation of the student body) and

- political context and policy goals (expansion of supply, broad quality improvement, boost excellence).

Such a system could help one compare 'apples with apples' regarding international university governance. The system could build on data that UNESCO has compiled, most recently in its report "Governance reforms in higher education: A study of institutional autonomy in Asian countries" (Varghese & Martin, 2013).

There is certainly no one-size-fits-all blueprint for good university governance, and the policy framework within which the tertiary institution is operating matters. Both the lack of diversity and the lack of cohesion in higher education strategies pose challenges. A reporting mechanism across countries and regions could increase understanding of what works well under which conditions and why. This could help universities and governments develop individual strategies for higher education reforms.

Recommendation

Examine university governance in global comparison.

It is difficult to compare university governance globally, because of very uneven legal contexts and reporting formats. The European Commission, together with UNESCO, should promote further research on good governance in tertiary education and why it works well in any particular context. This comparative learning exercise could include the US and China.

5. POLICY RECOMMENDATIONS FOR THE EU: LEARNING FROM CHINA AND THE US

The EU must remain competitive in the knowledge-based global economy by developing its talent pipeline. With this aim in mind, the EU and its member states should:

- conduct research into the state of human capital,

- create incentives to counteract a depletion of skills and to develop talent,

- make investments that increase the positive impact of competence on economies and societies and

- increase the relevance of tertiary education for the labour market and life chances.

Figure 16. Virtual circles in talent and education

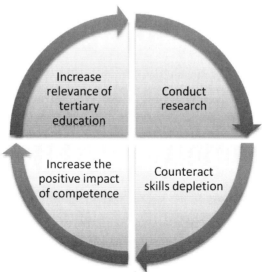

Source: Authors' own conceptualisation.

Such elements could be thought of as contributing to 'virtuous circles' of talent and innovation to sustain prosperity and growth. This report has analysed a number of indicators and policy trends and has distilled the following four proposals as to how the EU and its member states can create such virtuous circles.

5.1 Build a robust evidence-base regarding the state of human capital

The quality and quantity of education around the globe is changing rapidly. These changes will have a significant impact on the quality of life and economic health of countries around the world. Increasing the evidence-base surrounding higher education and examining the state of tertiary education in a global context will contribute to better policy-making in the EU and its member states. The EU and its member states can do this by:

Measuring the quantity of education in global comparison

The EU's tertiary education benchmark, which is embedded in the Europe 2020 strategy, aims to increase the tertiary graduation rate among 30- to 34-year olds to 40% in the EU. This benchmark should be reported on in the context of a *global comparison* and the progress of EU member states should be discussed regularly by the responsible ministers from EU member states in a global – and not just an intra-EU – comparison. Non-EU countries that are forecast to set the global benchmarks for graduating large skill cohorts, such as China, or those graduating a large percentage of their population from universities, such as Korea, could be referenced.

Improving transparency in university performance

The European Commission has provided seed funding for the multidimensional university assessment tool U-Multirank. This assessment tool has overcome some of the shortfalls of some university rankings. The Commission should work strongly with the private sector and foundations to ensure the longstanding operation of U-Multirank.

Benchmarking tertiary-educated persons around the globe

Although the OECD's AHELO project has encountered considerable challenges, assessing what university students know at the end of their undergraduate studies would be an important way to better understand the quality of human capital around the globe. Such a project might best be piloted regionally (to overcome the challenges of globally diverse learning and testing cultures) and could be developed in cooperation with at least one non-regional partner (such as the US or Canada). Once the feasibility of the tertiary knowledge evaluation is established, further regional pilots could be initiated and methods for comparing skill levels inter-regionally could be developed. Such a tool should evaluate generic skills, but could be expanded to examine discipline-specific skills. In the EU, the European Commission could consider fostering such an initiative.

Examining university governance in global comparison

It is difficult to compare university governance globally, because of very uneven legal contexts and reporting formats. The European Commission, together with UNESCO, should promote further research on good governance in tertiary education and why it works well in any particular context. This comparative learning exercise could include the US and China.

Better monitoring of advances in digital learning

The EU and its member states should support and monitor the digital learning initiatives of European institutions of higher education more strongly. Universities should summarise their digital learning activities as part of their standard institutional profile.

5.2 Create smart incentives to counteract skills depletion and to develop talent

Attracting and retaining talent will become a crucial part of the EU's economic policies in the future. The EU's higher education policy can form a cornerstone for an EU-wide talent strategy. For a continent in demographic decline, a contracting labour force in many EU countries poses a threat to innovation and economic prosperity in the region. The EU's predominantly knowledge-based economies will require a secure talent pipeline. The EU and its member states can achieve this by:

Preventing STEM-skill depletion

The EU, EU member states and the private sector have increased their efforts to encourage the development of STEM (science, technology, engineering and mathematics) skills, especially by fostering intra-EU projects. These initiatives should be expanded through exchanges beyond Europe. Countries such as China, India and the US, with large STEM programmes and skill cohorts, should be considered as partners with which to work with more strategically. Private-sector involvement in fostering STEM skill acquisition has two important components: ensuring that the skills acquired match current labour market standards and motivating students to learn skills that lead to promising employment opportunities by introducing them into workplaces during their studies.

Improving the mobility of non-EU graduates

The EU as a whole is more attractive to international students than any one of its member states is on its own. The EU should help European universities increase their appeal to non-EU students by introducing a Graduate Mobility Card, which would allow non-EU citizens who graduate from EU universities to look for employment in all EU member states for a period of time following the completion of their European degree.

5.3 Make investments that increase the positive impact of competence on economies and societies

Not only total investments, but smart and targeted investments are important to improving the positive impact that universities and graduates have on society. Tertiary graduates are becoming more interested in making the most of their investment in learning and new technology is changing the way in which education is delivered. The EU and its member states can make the most of skilled graduates by:

> *Increasing support and spending-efficiency for higher education, without crowding out the public sector*
>
> Funding tertiary education is a key responsibility of the state. While monitoring the impact of increased private support, the EU and its member states should create greater incentives for the private funding of education and increasingly profile best practices regarding spending efficiency by universities. This could be done through private-sector investments in R&D (to increase innovation), scholarships and internships (to increase access to learning) and programmes that help students make the transition from university to work (to find jobs that match their skills). Both the public and private sectors should work with universities to set targets and create incentives for the efficient use of higher education and research funding. For those institutions that set and meet 'smart spending targets', additional funding should be made available as part of an incentive system.
>
> *Fostering a 'client-based' and co-knowledge-production learning culture at universities*
>
> Learning cultures at universities can be very diverse, and too often students are not viewed as the universities' most important clients. Universities in the EU should find ways to become more service-oriented (such as increasing the academic advisory role of teachers and professors). They should also view students as co-producers of

knowledge and should foster such a culture both inside and outside the classroom.

Taking advantage of cross-institutional learning in the digital age

The European Credits System allows for the easy transfer of credits from one university to another. The EU and its member states should use its credit transferability advantage more strategically. Universities should examine how on- and offline learning models could be integrated to improve the quality and quantity of education. Public and private funding incentives in the EU and its member states should be examined to enable universities that have developed digital strategies to pursue these in greater scope.

5.4 Increase the relevance of tertiary education for the labour market and life chances

Matching skills with jobs is one of the biggest challenges the EU and its member states face as human capital becomes an increasingly scarce resource. The idea of having a large, highly skilled and young labour force in search of work will soon be confined to the history books in the EU. Once labour supply scarcity sets in, it will pose significant challenges that could unsettle economic security in the EU. The EU and its member states must work to ensure that skills and labour market needs do not deviate too greatly. This can be ensured by:

Improving job- and skills-matching

With an increasing proportion of the global population completing tertiary degrees, skills- and job-matching of graduates with appropriate jobs is becoming important to maintaining healthy economies. Market forces alone do not adequately match qualifications with employment opportunities. Students should be better informed about how their educational choices relate to employment through the incorporation of employability indicators in university rankings. Additionally, public and commercial skills and job-matching initiatives should be developed to create low-cost and efficient information portals that match employers with the talent they seek.

Using the knowledge and experiences of university alumni better

Universities should keep better track of the experiences of their alumni, especially their insights regarding looking for work. Building and maintaining alumni networks can benefit universities in many ways, and these networks can foster job-matching and help university leaders understand how well their curricula apply to labour markets.

The EU and its member states are edging towards a 'tipping point' in the global balance of human capital. The 'brain pool' is shifting towards Asian countries and with this change, the EU will have to modify its strategies and policies. This report has highlighted some of the coming challenges and has distilled policy options for the EU and its member states to maintain competitiveness in the region. The policy mix suggested in this report contains elements for creating 'virtuous circles' of talent and innovation to sustain prosperity and growth across the EU.

REFERENCES

Aalto University (2014), "Annual Report 2013", March (www.aalto.fi/en/about/reports_and_statistics/).

Acemoglu, D., P. Aghion, and F. Zilibotti (2006), "Distance to frontier, selection, and economic growth", *Journal of the European Economic Association*, No. 4, Vol. 1, pp. 37-74.

Aghion, P. (2008), "Higher Education and Innovation", *Perspektiven der Wirtschaftspolitik* No. 9, pp. 28-45.

Aghion, P. and P. Howitt (2006), "Appropriate Growth Policy: A Unifying Framework", *Journal of the European Economic Association*, Vol. 4, pp. 269-314.

Aghion, P., M. Dewatripont, C. Hoxby, A. Mas-Colell and A. Sapir (2007), "Why Reform Europe's Universities?", Bruegel Policy Brief No. 4, Bruegel, Brussels.

_____ (2008), "Higher aspirations: An agenda for reforming European universities", Bruegel Blueprint Series No. 5, Bruegel, Brussels.

_____ (2010), "The governance and performance of universities: Evidence from Europe and the US", *Economic Policy*, Vol. 1, pp. 7-59.

American Association of University Professors (2014), "Our Programs" (www.aaup.org/our-programs).

Auswertiges Amt (2012), "Zuwanderungsgesetz" (www.auswaertiges-amt.de/DE/EinreiseUndAufenthalt/Zuwanderungsrecht_node.html).

Barro and Lee (2013), "A new data set of educational attainment in the world 1950-2010", *Journal of Development Economics*, No. 104, pp. 184-198.

Battelle (2011), "R&D Magazine Annual Global Funding Forecast Predicts R&D Spending Growth will Continue While Globalization Accelerates" (www.battelle.org/media/press-releases/battelle-r-d-magazine-annual-global-funding-forecast-predicts-r-d-spending-growth-will-continue-while-globalization-accelerates).

Benhabib, J. and M. Spiegel (1994), "The role of human capital in economic development: Evidence from aggregate cross-country data", *Journal of Monetary Economics*, No. 39, pp. 143-173.

Böhm, A., M. Follari, A. Hewett, S. Jones, N. Kemp, D. Meares, D. Pearce and K. Van Cauter (2004), "Forecasting international student mobility - a UK perspective", British Council (www.britishcouncil.org/sites/britishcouncil.uk2/files/vision-2020.pdf).

Boston Consulting Group (2014), "The Global Workforce Crisis: $10 Trillion at Risk", Düsseldorf (www.bcgperspectives.com/content/articles/management_two_speed_economy_public_sector_global_workforce_crisis/?chapter=2).

Bundesministerium für Arbeit, Soziales, Konsumentenschutz, Bundesministerium für Inneres and Europa Integration Äusseres (2014), "Living and working in Austria" (www.migration.gv.at/en/types-of-immigration/permanent-immigration-red-white-red-card/skilled-workers-in-shortage-occupations.html#c2820).

Bundesministerium für Wirtschaft und Energie, Bundesministerium für Arbeit und Soziales and Bundesagentur für Arbeit (2014), "Make it in Germany" (www.make-it-in-germany.com/en/working/which-occupations-are-in-demand/).

Carneiro, P. and J. Heckman (2003), "Human Capital Policy", in James Heckman, Alan Krueger and Benjamin M. Friedman (eds), *Inequality in America: What Role for Human Capital Policy?*, Cambridge, MA: MIT Press.

Center for World-Class Universities of Shanghai Jiao Tong University (2014a), "The Academic Ranking of World Universities" (www.shanghairanking.com/).

_____ (2014b), "Methodology" (www.shanghairanking.com/ARWU-Methodology-2013.html).

Centre for Higher Education Policy Studies (2008), "Progress in higher education reform across Europe: Governance Reform" (http://www.utwente.nl/mb/cheps/publications/publications%202009/c9hdb101%20modern%20project%20report.pdf).

Chinese Education Reform (2010), "Outline of China's National Plan for Medium and Long-term Education Reform and Development (2010-2020)", Beijing.

Chinese Scholarship Council (2013), "Chinese Govt to Support 50,000 International Students in 2015" (www.csc.edu.cn/laihua/newsdetailen.aspx?cid=208&id=2339).

Consejo Superior de Investigaciones Científicas (2014), "Webometrics Ranking of World Universities" (www.webometrics.info/en).

Council of Europe (1997), "Convention on the Recognition of Qualifications concerning Higher Education in the European Region", CETS, No. 165 (http://conventions.coe.int/Treaty/Commun/QueVoulezVous.asp?NT=165&CM=8&DF=10/17/2007&CL=ENG).

Council of the European Union (2004), "Directive on the conditions of admission of third-country nationals for the purposes of studies, pupil exchange, unremunerated training or voluntary service", Council Directive 2005/71/EC, 13 December.

_____ (2005), "Directive on a specific procedure for admitting third-country nationals for the purposes of scientific research", Council Directive 2004/114/EC, 12 October.

_____ (2014), EDUC 132 SOC 308, 2 May, Brussels (http://register.consilium.europa.eu/doc/srv?l=EN&f=ST%209127%202014%20INIT).

Downes, M., Y. Wei and A. Zhou (2012), "Elite Universities in China and the Technology Sector: A Policy Analysis Report" (http://sites.fordschool.umich.edu/china-policy/files/2012/09/UTF-8Elite-Universities-in-China-A-Policy-Analysis-Report-Downes-Wei-Zhou.pdf).

Economist (The) (2014), "Crowning the dragon", 30 April (www.economist.com/blogs/graphicdetail/2014/04/daily-chart-19).

Embassy of Switzerland in China (2014), "Massive Open Online Courses (MOOCs) in China", European University Association, January (http://static.squarespace.com/static/507b7901e4b0954f51d4b097/t/5327c214e4b05d171abbc584/1395114516306/MOOCS%20in%20China.pdf).

Estermann, T., T. Nokkala and M. Steinel (2011), "University Autonomy in Europe II - The Scoreboard", European University Association (www.eua.be/eua-work-and-policy-area/governance-autonomy-and-funding.aspx).

European Commission (2008), "Higher Education Governance in Europe" (http://eacea.ec.europa.eu/education/eurydice/thematic_reports_en.php).

_____ (2010a), "Europe 2020 – A strategy for smart, sustainable and inclusive growth", COM(2010) 2020 final, Brussels, 3 March.

_____ (2010b), "Lisbon Strategy evaluation document", SEC(2010) 114 final, Brussels, 02.02.2010.

_____ (2011), "National Reform Programmes 2011" (http://ec.europa.eu/economy_finance/economic_governance/sgp/convergence/programmes/2011_en.htm).

_____ (2014a), "European Commission launches network to foster web talent through Massive Open Online Courses (MOOCs)", IP/14/335 27/03/2014 (http://europa.eu/rapid/press-release_IP-14-335_en.htm).

_____ (2014b), "European MOOCs Scoreboard" (www.openeducationeuropa.eu/en/european_scoreboard_moocs).

_____ (2014c), "ERA Progress Report 2013" (http://ec.europa.eu/research/era/index_en.htm).

_____ (2014d), "University Business Cooperation" (http://ec.europa.eu/education/tools/university-business_en.htm).

_____ (2014e), "Opening up education through new technologies", DG Education (http://ec.europa.eu/education/policy/strategic-framework/education-technology_en.htm).

European University Association (2014), "Governance, Autonomy and Funding" (www.eua.be/eua-work-and-policy-area/governance-autonomy-and-funding.aspx).

Eurostat (2014a), "Headline indicators – Europe 2020" (http://epp.eurostat.ec.europa.eu/portal/page/portal/europe_2020_indicators/headline_indicators).

_____ (2014b), "General government expenditure by function" (http://epp.eurostat.ec.europa.eu/statistics_explained/index.php /Government_expenditure_by_function_%E2%80%93_COFOG).

Federal Ministry of Education and Research (Germany) (2014), "The European Research Area (ERA)" (www.bmbf.de/en/956.php).

Forestier, K. (2013), "China's new MOOCs could be a double-edged sword", *University World News*, 1 November, No. 294 (www.universityworldnews.com/article.php?story=201311011546 20288).

Gaebel, M. (2013), "MOOCs", EUA Presentation, European University Association, Brussels (www.slideshare.net/Kolds/gaebel2013-06-20-madison-moocs).

_____ (2014), "MOOCs", EUA Occasional Paper, European University Association, Brussels, January (www.eua.be/Libraries/Publication/MOOCs_Update_January_2 014.sflb.ashx).

Gereffi, G., V. Wadhwa, B. Rissing and R. Ong (2008), "Getting the Numbers Right: International engineering education in the United States, China, and India", *Journal of Engineering Education,* Vol. 97, No. 1, pp. 13-25.

Gros, D. and C. Alcidi (2013), *The Global Economy in 2030 - Trends and Strategies for Europe*, CEPS Paperback, Centre for European Policy Studies, Brussels (www.ceps.eu/book/global-economy-2030-trends-and-strategies-europe-0).

Hu, Y. (2013), "Oversupply of College Graduates? Structural Mismatch!", Peterson Institute for International Economics, Washington, D.C. (http://blogs.piie.com/china/?p=2876).

Gereffi, G. (2008), "International Engineering Education in the United States, China and India", *Journal of Engineering* Education, Vol. 1, pp. 13-25.

International Ranking Expert Group (2006), "Berlin Principles on Ranking of Higher Education Institutions" (www.ireg-observatory.org/index.php?option=com_content&task=view&id= 41&Itemid=48).

Brücker, H., A. Hauptmann and E. Vallizadeh (2012), "Zuwanderer aus Bulgarien und Rumänien - Arbeitsmigration oder Armutsmigration?", IAB Kurzbericht 16/2013 (doku.iab.de/kurzber/2013/kb1613.pdf).

Jiang, K. (2011), "De-bureaucratization within China's Universities", *Inside Higher Ed*, 12 February (www.insidehighered.com/blogs/the_world_view/de_bureaucra tization_within_china_s_universities#sthash.URXIbqTW.VkGvbm TM.dpbs).

Jong-Wha, L. (2014), "China's Education Revolution", Project Syndicate, (www.project-syndicate.org/commentary/lee-jong-wha-emphasizes-the-need-for-more-accessible--higher-quality-secondary-and-tertiary-programs).

Juno, M. (2011), "Public spending and university quality: Is there a link?", QS Intelligence Unit (www.iu.qs.com/2011/12/public-spending-and-university-quality-is-there-a-link/).

Kiwana, L., A. Kumar and N. Randerson (2012), "The skills 'threat' from China and India – Fact or Fiction?", *Engineering U.K.*, March.

KKR Insights (2012), "Global Macro Trends" (www.kkr.com/company/insights/global-macro-trends-16).

Li, Y., J. Walley, Z. Shan and X. Zhao (2008), "The Higher Educational Transformation of China and its Global Implications", NBER Working Paper Series, No. 13849, National Bureau of Economic Research, Cambridge, MA.

Lombardi, J.V., C.W. Abbey and D.D. Craig (2011), "The Top American Research Universities: 2011 Annual Report", Lumina Foundation, The Center for Measuring University Performance at Arizona State University, Phoenix, AZ.

Min, H. (2011), "The reform and development of higher education in China", 17 May, Beijing University (www.emeuropeasia.org/upload/EMECW11/Conf_HAN_MIN_MoE.pdf).

Ministry of Education of the People's Republic of China (2010), "List of Chinese Higher Education Institutions", 30 July (www.moe.edu.cn/publicfiles/business/htmlfiles/moe/moe_286 2/201010/109031.html).

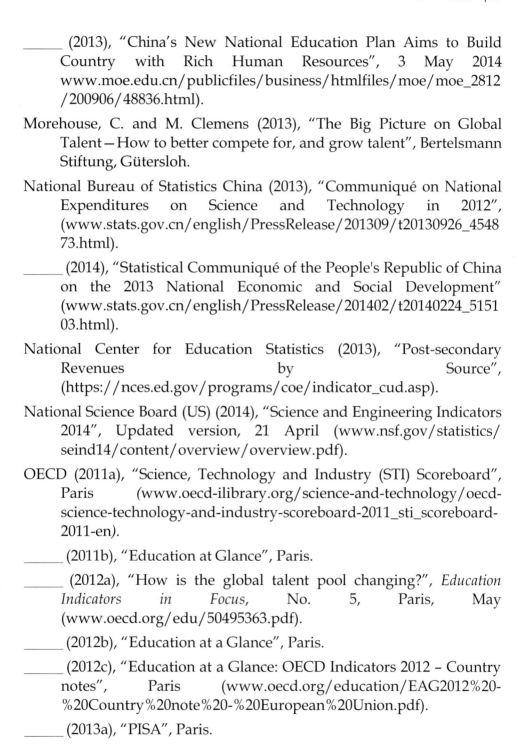

_____ (2013), "China's New National Education Plan Aims to Build Country with Rich Human Resources", 3 May 2014 www.moe.edu.cn/publicfiles/business/htmlfiles/moe/moe_2812 /200906/48836.html).

Morehouse, C. and M. Clemens (2013), "The Big Picture on Global Talent — How to better compete for, and grow talent", Bertelsmann Stiftung, Gütersloh.

National Bureau of Statistics China (2013), "Communiqué on National Expenditures on Science and Technology in 2012", (www.stats.gov.cn/english/PressRelease/201309/t20130926_4548 73.html).

_____ (2014), "Statistical Communiqué of the People's Republic of China on the 2013 National Economic and Social Development" (www.stats.gov.cn/english/PressRelease/201402/t20140224_5151 03.html).

National Center for Education Statistics (2013), "Post-secondary Revenues by Source", (https://nces.ed.gov/programs/coe/indicator_cud.asp).

National Science Board (US) (2014), "Science and Engineering Indicators 2014", Updated version, 21 April (www.nsf.gov/statistics/ seind14/content/overview/overview.pdf).

OECD (2011a), "Science, Technology and Industry (STI) Scoreboard", Paris (www.oecd-ilibrary.org/science-and-technology/oecd-science-technology-and-industry-scoreboard-2011_sti_scoreboard-2011-en).

_____ (2011b), "Education at Glance", Paris.

_____ (2012a), "How is the global talent pool changing?", _Education Indicators in Focus_, No. 5, Paris, May (www.oecd.org/edu/50495363.pdf).

_____ (2012b), "Education at a Glance", Paris.

_____ (2012c), "Education at a Glance: OECD Indicators 2012 – Country notes", Paris (www.oecd.org/education/EAG2012%20-%20Country%20note%20-%20European%20Union.pdf).

_____ (2013a), "PISA", Paris.

_____ (2013b), "OECD Skills Outlook 2013. First Results of the survey of Adult Skills", Paris.

_____ (2013c), "Education at a Glance", Paris.

_____ (2014), "Is migration really increasing?", Migration Policy Debates No. 1, Paris, May.

OpenupEd (2014), "OpenupED" (www.openuped.eu/).

Quacquarelli Symonds (QS) (2014a), "QS World University Rankings" (www.topuniversities.com/qs-world-university-rankings).

_____ (2014b), "Ranking Indicators" (www.iu.qs.com/university-rankings/rankings-indicators/).

Rauhvargers, A. (2011), "Global University Rankings and Their Impact", EUA Report on Rankings 2011, European University Association, Brussels.

_____ (2013), "Global University Rankings and their impact. Report II", European University Association, Brussels.

Saisana, M., B. d'Hombres and A. Saltelli (2011), "Rickety numbers: Volatility of university rankings and policy implications", *Research Policy*, No. 40, pp. 165-177.

Sapir, A., P. Aghion, G. Bertola, M. Hellwig, J. Pisani Ferry, D. Rosati, J. Vinals and H. Wallace (2004), *An Agenda for growing Europe,* Oxford: Oxford University Press.

SEI (2012), Science and Engineering Indicators 2012, (US) National Science Foundation, Washington, D.C. (www.nsf.gov/statistics/seind12/figures_tn1.htm).

Times Higher Education (2014a), "World University Rankings" (www.timeshighereducation.co.uk/world-university-rankings/2013-14/world-ranking).

_____ (2014b), "World University Rankings 2013-2014 methodology" (www.timeshighereducation.co.uk/world-university-rankings/2013-14/world-ranking/methodology).

Timmer, M., R. Inklaar, M. O'Mahony and B. van Ark (2010), *Economic Growth in Europe*, Cambridge: Cambridge University Press.

Tremblay, K., D. LaLancette and D. Roseveare (2012), "Assessment of Higher Education Learning Outcome (AHELO) - Feasibility Study Report", OECD, Paris.

UK Department of Visas and Immigration (2014), "Tier 2 Shortage Occupation List" (www.gov.uk/government/uploads/system/uploads/attachment_data/file/261493/shortageoccupationlistnov11.pdf).

Van Ark, B., M. O'Mahony and M.P. Timmer (2008), "The Productivity Gap between Europe and the United States: Trends and Causes", *Journal of Economic Perspectives,* No. 22, Vol. 1, pp. 25-44.

Van Damme, D. (2013), "Cutting education expenditure", OECD, 23 December (http://oecdeducationtoday.blogspot.de/2013/12/cutting-education-expenditure.html).

Vandenbussche, J., P. Aghion and C. Meghir (2006), "Growth, Distance to Frontier and Composition of Human Capital", *Journal of Economic Growth*, No. 11, pp. 97-127.

Varghese, N. and M. Martin (2013), "Governance reforms in higher education: A study of institutional autonomy in Asian countries", International Institute for Educational Planning, UNESCO (www.iiep.unesco.org/fileadmin/user_upload/Info_Services_Publications/pdf/2013/Gov_reform_in_HE_Asia.pdf).

Wang, G. (2010), "China's Higher Education Reform", China Research Center, Vol. 9, No. 1 (www.chinacenter.net/chinas-higher-education-reform/).

World Bank (2013), Worldwide Governance Indicators (http://data.worldbank.org/data-catalog/worldwide-governance-indicators).

World Economic Forum (2014), "Global Competitiveness Index" (www3.weforum.org/docs/GCR2013-14/GCR_Rankings_2013-14.pdf).

ANNEX. MEMBERS OF THE CEPS TASK FORCE AND INVITED SPEAKERS

Göran Bäckblom, VP Public Affairs and Corporate Advisor Business and Technology Development, Luossavaara-Kiirunavaara AB (LKAB)

Mikkel Barslund, Research Fellow, CEPS

Frederique Biston, Senior Vice President, EU Office, Volvo AB

Kerstin Born-Sirkel, Director of Corporate and External Relations, CEPS

Matthias Busse, Task Force Rapporteur and Researcher, CEPS

Maria Da Graça Carvalho, MEP (EPP), Member of the Committee on Industry, Research and Energy, European Parliament

Rasmus Dahl, Consultant, Confederation of Danish Industry - DI

Marc Durando, Executive Director, European Schoolnet

Ulla Engelmann, Head of Unit, DG JRC, European Commission

Sophia Eriksson Waterschoot, Adviser to the Deputy Director General, DG EAC, European Commission

Gero Federkeil, Project Leader U – Multirank, Centre for Higher Education

Harald Gruber, Head of Division, European Investment Bank - EIB

Staffan Jerneck, Senior Adviser, CEPS

Elpida Keravnou-Papailiou, Rector, Cyprus University of Technology, and Governing Board Member, European Institute of Innovation and Technology

Kimberley Lansford, Senior Policy Adviser, European Round Table of Industrialists

Ilaria Maselli, Researcher, Economic Policy Unit, CEPS

Christal Morehouse, Task Force Rapporteur and Senior Project Manager, Bertelsmann Foundation

Diana Musteata, Administrative and Marketing Assistant, CEPS

Maria Helena Nazaré, President, European University Association

Marianne Paasi, Scientific Officer, DG RTD, European Commission

Xavier Prats Monné, Deputy Director General, DG EAC, European Commission

Dominique Ristori, Director General, DG JRC, European Commission

Felix Roth, Research Fellow and Editor of Intereconomics, CEPS

Andrea Saltelli, Head of Unit, DG JRC, European Commission

Christian Schutz, Head of Global University Relations, Corporate Human Resources, University Relations Intranet Page, Siemens AG

Stephen Stacey, Director and Executive Representative, Hyundai Motor Company

Jan-Eric Sundgren, Senior Adviser to the CEO, Volvo

Anna-Elisabeth Thum, Research Fellow, CEPS

Takahiro Tomonaga, General Manager, Mitsui & Co. Benelux

Adam Tyson, Head of Higher Education: Modernisation Agenda, Erasmus, DG Education and Culture, European Commission

Filip Van Depoele, Advisor to the Deputy Director-General, European Commission

Peter Van Der Hijden, Policy Officer, DG RTD, European Commission

Marijk van der Wende, Dean, Amsterdam University College

Daniel Vertesy, Econometrics and Applied Statistics, Joint Research Centre, European Commission

Patricia Wastiau, Principal Advisor for Research and Studies, European Schoolnet

INDEX